Cambridge Elements ☰

Elements in the Gothic
edited by
Dale Townshend
Manchester Metropolitan University
Angela Wright
University of Sheffield

DICKENS AND THE GOTHIC

Andrew Smith
University of Sheffield

CAMBRIDGE
UNIVERSITY PRESS

CAMBRIDGE
UNIVERSITY PRESS

Shaftesbury Road, Cambridge CB2 8EA, United Kingdom

One Liberty Plaza, 20th Floor, New York, NY 10006, USA

477 Williamstown Road, Port Melbourne, VIC 3207, Australia

314–321, 3rd Floor, Plot 3, Splendor Forum, Jasola District Centre, New Delhi – 110025, India

103 Penang Road, #05–06/07, Visioncrest Commercial, Singapore 238467

Cambridge University Press is part of Cambridge University Press & Assessment, a department of the University of Cambridge.

We share the University's mission to contribute to society through the pursuit of education, learning and research at the highest international levels of excellence.

www.cambridge.org
Information on this title: www.cambridge.org/9781009539104

DOI: 10.1017/9781009282512

First published 2024

A catalogue record for this publication is available from the British Library.

ISBN 978-1-009-53910-4 Hardback
ISBN 978-1-009-28247-5 Paperback
ISSN 2634-8721 (online)
ISSN 2634-8713 (print)

Cambridge University Press & Assessment has no responsibility for the persistence or accuracy of URLs for external or third-party internet websites referred to in this publication and does not guarantee that any content on such websites is, or will remain, accurate or appropriate.

Dickens and the Gothic

Elements in the Gothic

DOI: 10.1017/9781009282512
First published online: June 2024

Andrew Smith
University of Sheffield
Author for correspondence: Andrew Smith, Andrew.smith1@sheffield.ac.uk

Abstract: *Dickens and the Gothic* provides a critical focus on representations of social and psychological entrapment which demonstrates how Dickens employs the Gothic to evaluate how institutions and formations of history impinge on the individual. An analysis of these forms of Gothic entrapment reveals how these institutions and representations of public and personal history function Gothically in Dickens, because they hold back other, putatively reformist, ambitions. To be trapped in an institution such as a prison, or by the machinations of a law court, or haunted by history, or to be haunted by ghosts, represent forms of Gothic entrapment which this study examines both psychologically and sociologically.

Keywords: Dickens, Gothic, ghost story, prisons, Victorian literature

ISBNs: 9781009539104 (HB), 9781009282475 (PB), 9781009282512 (OC)
ISSNs: 2634-8721 (online), 2634-8713 (print)

Contents

Introduction

Dickens' *Sketches by Boz* (1836), includes a Gothic tale, 'The Black Veil'. The tale is set in 1800 and centres on a young doctor who is approached one rainy winter evening by a tall mysterious woman, dressed in black with her face concealed behind the eponymous veil. This figure asks the unnamed surgeon to attend her on the following evening when she will possibly have a recently deceased patient in her care who will require immediate medical attention which may restore them to life. The doctor asks why it is not possible to see the patient immediately so that they can intervene before the patient's health takes a critical turn, but the mysterious woman indicates that she does not currently have access to the patient and therefore the doctor will need to wait until the following morning. The doctor is struck by the impossible demand (that he attempt to revive a corpse rather than assist before death), but agrees to it out of some tacit concerns about the health of the woman who is either 'mad', or possibly aware of an intended murder taking place the following morning in which 'the timely interposition of medical aid', might save the victim.[1]

The doctor has 'a sleepless night' in which 'he was unable to banish the black veil from his disturbed imagination' (p. 363). The following morning he makes his way to a desolate part of Walworth, described as 'a dreary waste' (p. 363), populated by the ruins of cottages 'fast falling to pieces with decay and neglect' (p. 363). The address leads him to 'a small low building, one story above the ground, with even a more desolate and unpromising exterior than any he had yet passed' (p. 364). He is greeted at the door by 'a tall, ill-favoured man, with black hair, and a face . . . as pale and haggard as the countenance of any dead man he ever saw' (p. 365), who lets him into the building. The doctor finds the veiled woman who conducts him to a room in which he discovers a corpse lying on the bed. The corpse exhibits signs of violence which identifies strangulation as the cause of death. He concludes that he is indeed looking at the murder victim that he had anticipated from the night before, a view that the woman seemingly corroborates when she cries out that he has been 'piteously, inhumanly murdered!' (p. 367). The surgeon soon realises that the man has been executed and that the body is that of the woman's son. It transpires that the woman was a friendless impoverished widow who had made numerous sacrifices to help her young son, only for him to fall into a life of crime which had resulted in 'his own death by the hangman's hands' which provokes 'his mother shame, and incurable insanity' (p. 367). The surgeon, moved by her story, becomes a frequent

---

[1] Charles Dickens, 'The Black Veil' in Michael Slater (ed.), *Dickens' Journalism: Sketches by Boz and Other Early Papers 1833–39* (London: Dent, 1996), pp. 359–68, p. 363. Further reference to this tale will be inserted parenthetically in the text.

visitor to 'the harmless mad woman' (p. 367) and provides her with psychological and financial support for the rest of her life.

'The Black Veil' evokes images from an earlier Gothic tradition which is suggested by its 1800 setting and foregrounding of a black veil, which echoes the black veils found by Emily St. Aubert in Radcliffe's *The Mysteries of Udolpho* (1794), which are associated with death, decay, and mystery. Behind one such veil Emily seems to find a rotting corpse, which is revealed to be a waxwork. This way of undoing a Gothic mystery, in which things are not as they seem, is inherited by Dickens. The pervasive mood of grief in his tale and the possible presence of providential reward are also evocative of Radcliffe. The dying mother, in her final moments, prays thanks to God for the doctor's support after which 'The prayer flew to Heaven, and was heard' (p. 368), so that the doctor was 'repaid a thousandfold' with public honours and enhanced professional standing, although for him he has no memory 'more gratifying to his heart than that connected with The Black Veil' (p. 368). We can see, however, that Dickens, while drawing upon an older Gothic tradition, wants to move the Gothic in a new direction. The sublime foreign landscapes of Radcliffe are replaced by the slums of Walworth. There might be suggestions of some form of providence in the doctor's reward, but it is seemingly bad luck which has led to the son's execution when it is noted that 'A companion, equally guilty with himself, had been acquitted for want of evidence; and this man had been left for death, and been executed' (p. 367). Justice, in its human guise, therefore seems random and destructive. Dickens here sketches an idea about justice and the law which would be more fully elaborated in later works such as *Bleak House* (1853) and *Great Expectations* (1861). He is also sympathetically exploring the psychological consequences of forms of emotional and economic deprivation. The narrator of 'The Black Veil' notes of the woman's finally revealed face, that it was 'deadly pale; and there was a nervous contortion to the lip, and an unnatural fire in her eye, which showed too plainly that her bodily and mental powers had nearly sunk beneath an accumulation of misery' (p. 367). There is an emerging reformist Dickens here in a tale which centres on the consequences of forms of social and economic deprivation. At the end of the tale, the dramatic focus shifts towards the empathetic doctor as the only source of emotional solace in a world governed by poverty, injustice, misery, and madness. In short, his compassion might be the antidote to the Gothic gloom and within that compassion a reformist impulse is discernable.

Michael Hollington has examined the debt that Dickens owes to an earlier Radcliffean Gothic tradition in *Sketches by Boz* where Dickens linked the Gothic to his agenda for social reform. Hollington notes that Dickens connects Radcliffe to the social reformer Elizabeth Fry, whose interest in the treatment of criminals clearly appealed to Dickens. Dickens in 'Criminal Courts' (published in *Sketches*, although first published as 'Old Bailey' in the *Morning Chronicle* in 1834), notes, after a glimpse of the horrors of Newgate Prison, that 'We have a great respect for Mrs Fry, but she certainly ought to have written more romances than Mrs Radcliffe'.[2] To that end Hollington identifies an ambition in *Sketches* to awaken the reader to the social horrors of modern life and in order to 'emancipate' them from 'the deep indifference' engendered by 'modern city life', just as Radcliffe had also sought to challenge forms of social injustice in her Gothic novels.[3]

Robert Mighall, following Hollington's lead, has explored 'Dickens's Reformist Gothic' and persuasively argued that Dickens used the Gothic in order to identify how historical forces curb social progress.[4] This, however, is only part of the story, and this study of the Gothic re-examines the relationship between social reform and the Gothic by moving beyond the predominant focus on the past in order to address how Gothic images of incarceration, and psychological states, are employed by Dickens to reflect on additional barriers to social reform. We will also see how the Gothic shapes tensions between freedoms of literary expression and rhetorical modes of entrapment (a notable feature of *The Pickwick Papers* (1837), which is discussed below). Throughout Dickens' writing the Gothic repeatedly appears as a block to reformist thinking and this is developed in psychological, emotional, linguistic, and disciplinary contexts as well as in reflections upon history.

Dickens' ambition is to inform the reader about the need for reform and, as in 'The Black Veil', to make the reader become like the doctor, who is initially baffled by his visitor, then intrigued and finally fully engaged with their plight. The aim is to cast off a Gothic world which is physically and socially present but also registered through psychological affect. This turn towards the inner life represents, as we shall see, a particularly complex formation of the Gothic which anticipates a Freudian uncanny in which doubled selves constitute moments of psychological entrapment. In Dickens, places of correction (most notably prisons) also function as sites of physical confinement which are employed to explore the mental states generated by claustrophobic spaces. What holds the subject back from seeing the human reality beneath a blasted social world, and so becoming a reformer, is a series of obstacles (institutions,

---

[2] Charles Dickens, 'Criminal Courts' in Michael Slater (ed.), *Dickens' Journalism: Sketches by Boz and Other Early Papers, 1833–39* (London: Dent, 1996), pp. 194–98, p. 195.

[3] Michael Hollington, 'Boz's Gothic Gargoyles', *Dickens Quarterly*, 1999, Vol. 16, No. 3: 160–77, (p. 163).

[4] Robert Mighall, 'Dickens and the Gothic' in David Paroissien (ed.), *Companion to Charles Dickens* (Hoboken: Wiley-Blackwell, 2008), pp. 81–96, p. 86.

but also mindsets) which constitute moments of blockage that are rendered in specifically Gothic terms. The Gothic thus indicates the place, or type of institution, where social reform is needed. If these obstacles are removed then, as in 'The Black Veil', the Gothic disappears (indeed, in that instance becomes overwritten by heavenly reward).

There have been studies, such as Mighall's (1999, 2008), which have explored Dickens' important role in ushering in a new form of urban Gothic, which also raised questions about social reform. Other studies have explored Dickens' debt to the earlier eighteenth-century Gothic, of Radcliffe and others, which he mined for his representations of villains and to draw upon many of the features of a Female Gothic tradition (most notably present in *Bleak House*) (See Milbank 1992). Whilst this study will explore many of these critical contexts, it is important to note that the principal argument is that the origins of Dickens' reformist Gothic can be found in other places including within language, and specifically in his development of an innovative writing about the Gothic that generates a new way of thinking about institutions and the mindsets with which they are associated. Hollington touches on the importance of writing when he acknowledges that Dickens' radicalism is manifested out of forms of allegory.[5] Allegorical representation is both 'unreal' and insistently didactic. For Hollington, Michael Camille's account of how medieval marginalia critically writes back to the main text (as a type of subversion of the language of religious orthodoxy) stands as a conceit for how Dickens developed a particular type of Gothic writing which similarly critiques orthodox forms of expression, including existing forms of the Gothic. Some of these interventions are superficially playful as in Dickens' use of puns (Lady Dedlock in *Bleak House*, to give just one example, dies of exposure both literally and metaphorically). For Hollington the 'aim and effect of punning and language-deformation ... is to lay bare through the telling of suppressed and hidden "new Gothic" narratives the strangeness and cruelty of the modern metropolis'.[6] This seemingly playful language becomes co-opted to support the Gothic reformist cause as it creates a defamiliarisation that draws attention to the site where forms of social power and exploitation are both manifested and seemingly playfully hidden. As we shall see, to understand Dickens' Gothic it is important to pay attention to tone as well as structure and content.

'The Black Veil' feels like a conventional Gothic story which invites the reader to contemplate the horror of state murder. Telling the story of 'The Black Veil' is part of its unfolding as the tale both evokes an earlier Gothic tradition of story-telling and moves beyond it to generate a new formation of

[5] Hollington, 'Gargoyles', p. 163.   [6] Hollington, 'Gargoyles', p. 163.

the Gothic centred on modern forms of horror in which depersonalisation (neither the narrator, nor the mother, are named) transforms a specific plight into a more general social problem. That the importance of *how* the tale is told is crucial to Dickens is clear from those tales that directly address the significance of story-telling.[7] This form of self-reflection frequently occurs in his Gothic tales and contributes to the types of confinement which elsewhere are associated with physical and mental forms of confinement. His 'Nurse's Stories' from *The Uncommercial Traveller* (1860–61) provides an example of how these issues of confinement are reflected in linguistic forms of confinement.

The opening of 'Nurse's Stories' emphasises the importance of the imagination and imaginary places which can be repeatedly revisited, 'There are not many places that I find it more agreeable to revisit when I am in an idle mood, than some places to which I have never been'.[8] The literary text enables this, with reference made to the imaginary worlds created by Crusoe and Cervantes. The narrator reflects on the childhood tales told to them by their nurse, who begins by recounting a story based on Bluebeard, about a Captain Murderer who murders his young brides and bakes them in a pie and eats them. He meets his comeuppance after marrying the twin sister of a bride that he murders. The twin takes her revenge by poisoning herself on the eve of her murder so that he dies after eating the pie and consuming the poison that is within her. The tale serves as a sort of taster for the following tale which centres on a family of shipwrights, all called Chips, all of whom have sold their souls to the devil for 'an iron pot and a bushel of tenpenny nails and half a ton of copper and a rat that could speak' (p. 176). John Bowen has noted of the tale that it constitutes 'a compulsively repetitious story about compulsive repetition, which leads only to death and yet more repetition'.[9] Several generations of Chips have struck the same bargain, and the current descendent is approached by the devil who taunts him with the repeated refrain:

> 'A Lemon has pips,
> And a yard has ships,
> And *I'*ll have Chips!' (p. 176).

---

[7] Robert Mighall notes that Dickens refers to this as streaky Bacon, 'Dickens and the Gothic' (p. 82) in *Oliver Twist* (1838) as a way of referencing the different layers of writing (melodrama, tragedy, comedy) which also run alongside his use of the Gothic.

[8] Charles Dickens, 'Nurse's Stories' in Michael Slater and John Drew (eds.), *Dickens' Journalism: The Uncommercial Traveller and Other papers 1859–70* (London: Dent, 2000), pp. 169–80, p. 171. Further reference to this item will be inserted parenthetically in the text.

[9] John Bowen, 'Charles Dickens and the Gothic' in Dale Townshend and Angela Wright (eds.), *The Cambridge History of the Gothic: Gothic in the Nineteenth Century* (Cambridge: Cambridge University Press, 2020), pp. 246–64, p. 262.

Chips does not respond to this but the talking rat (which he has presumably inherited from his father) taunts him with the refrain after Chips had tried to kill it in a kettle of hot pitch. Chips' subsequent journey to the West Indies is brought to an end when a number of rats eat through the wooden hold of the ship and it sinks. Chips' body floats towards the shore with the talking rat sitting on it, from where it declaims:

> 'A Lemon has pips,
> And a yard has ships,
> And *I*'ve got Chips!' (p. 176).

These tales may seem far removed from the emerging reformist agenda that underpins 'The Black Veil', however, the Gothic in these tales constitutes a parallel, predominately linguistic, form of confinement which Dickens else-where uses to address social problems. In 'The Black Veil' the Gothic, as we have seen, is used to draw attention to forms of social deprivation which limit the lives of those residing in communities such as Walworth. In 'Nurse's Stories' the issue of confinement is displaced into the language of the second tale which suggests that Chips cannot escape as he is linguistically trapped within the repeated refrain of the story. The message of the tale is about inescapability. Chips cannot escape from the taunting verses as he cannot escape from the rats. Bowen relates this issue of repetition to the wider issues that characterise Dickens' work 'Much of the power of Dickens's texts stems from repetition – lexical, syntactical, grammatical, familial, paternal, and narrative – a repetition charged with a kind of diabolical energy that the texts seek simul-taneously to accelerate, exorcise and master: Gothic on speed'.[10] It is this type of rapid repetition which in turn generates a version of the uncanny, which also functions as a form of psychological containment in which the subject is confronted by versions of themselves, often in the form of the double, from which they cannot escape because uncanny forms of repetition generate 'that class of the frightening which leads back to what is known of old and long familiar'.[11] The use of literary language is important here as Freud also acknowledges that his study of the uncanny is about aesthetics when 'aesthetics is understood to mean not merely the theory of beauty but the theory of qualities of feeling'.[12] Mighall has noted how in *Great Expectations* Dickens developed a version of the subject (Pip) who has become emotionally lost and that within these 'Gothic imaginings' we witness 'The domain that

---

[10] Bowen, 'Charles Dickens and the Gothic', p. 263.

[11] Sigmund Freud, 'The Uncanny' in Albert Dickson (ed.), *Art and Literature: Jensen's 'Gradiva', Leonardo Da Vinci and Other Works* (Harmondsworth: Penguin, 1990), pp. 339–76, p. 340.

[12] Freud, 'The Uncanny', p. 330.

Freud would come to claim as his own',[13] although in *A Geography of Victorian Gothic Fiction* (1999) Mighall expresses some scepticism about psychological approaches to literature because such 'essentialist models encourage the suppression of history'.[14] This study is not a Freudian one, but it does, when relevant, as above, explore parallels between Freud's work on the uncanny and the type of psychological states, and models of the double, that we find in Dickens' writings especially when they are employed to reflect on states of confinement which are also articulated in rhetorical and linguistic forms. The language of story-telling, for example, identifies another place of confinement because of the way that the subject is psychologically 'trapped' within such language. That this issue of confinement is to a significant degree linguistic (although with consequences for psychological states) is also clear from some of the interpolated narratives about confinement that we find in the otherwise comic *The Pickwick Papers*.

Steven Marcus has noted how forms of confinement which characterise the inset tales in *The Pickwick Papers* work against the playful freedoms of language which are explored in the main plot. For Marcus, the principal narrative of the novel is exuberantly developed as it unshackles itself from pre-existing novelistic conventions. *The Pickwick Papers* represents a turning point in the development of the novel because in its linguistic play, 'Dickens was able to abandon himself or give expression to what Freud called the primary process in a degree that was unprecedented in English fictional prose', whereas previously such freedom of language had been predominately associated with poetry.[15] For Marcus this language use included the 'nonlogical' employment of metaphor and metonymy which created 'a new dimension of freedom for the English novel, if not for the human mind in general'.[16] New forms of literary expression and new formations of psychology are thus closely correlated but this is paralleled by another form of writing which inhabits the novel which is darker, constricted, and Gothic. Many of the interpolated tales are ghost stories, with some comic narratives which also evidence forms of confinement. Marcus has noted of these tales, that:

> In them motion and movement of both language and event come to a dead halt.
> In almost every one of them, even the funny ones, someone is paralyzed,

[13] Mighall, 'Dickens and the Gothic', p. 94.

[14] Robert Mighall, *A Geography of Victorian Gothic Fiction: Mapping History's Nightmares* (Oxford: Oxford University Press, 1999), p. 261.

[15] Steven Marcus, 'Language into Structure: Pickwick Revisited', *Daedalus*, Winter 1972, Vol. 101, No. 1, 183–202 (p. 189).

[16] Marcus, 'Pickwick Revisited', pp. 189, 190.

immobilized, or locked up and imprisoned in something. Their language is not
the free, wild, astonishingly creative language of the balance of the novel.[17]

In the novel, 'The Story of the Bagman's Uncle' provides an example of this.
The tale centres on how a Bagman (a collector of orders and samples, for
a fictitious clothing company called Tiggin and Welps) dreams that he is in
a carriage from where he helps an abducted women escape from two men, and
after fighting them he awakens. The romantic vision of the woman means that
he has never married because he could not find anyone who compared to her –
which prompted him in the dream to swear an oath of allegiance to her. In the
dream he is a romantic hero, in life he is not. His inability to cast off the dream
has led to an unnecessarily lonely life which has been socially, economically,
and emotionally confined as he is still on the road in pursuit of his livelihood.
The dream vision of romance leads not to escape but to isolation, in short, the
consequences of the dream turn it into a type of nightmare despite the fact that
the Uncle appears happy with his lot because 'He remained staunch to the great
oath he had sworn to the beautiful young lady: Refusing several eligible
landladies on her account, and died a bachelor at last'.[18] At one level the tale
revels in the freedoms of the single life as a way of reflecting on Pickwick's
predicament when Martha Bardwell brings a suit against him for breach of
promise, after which he is put in jail when he fails to pay the fine. The tone of the
story is also comic rather than Gothic and the Bagman's Uncle is represented as
an exuberant bon viveur, who in the end, 'at last', had managed to escape the
confines of marriage. It is in these moments that we witness a type of uncanny
doubling at work which occurs at a specifically generic level as the tale develops
tensions between comedy and the Gothic. The key issue, which moves the tale
towards the type of Gothic confinement that Marcus notes in such narratives, is
that the tale is the consequence of an alcohol-fueled dream. For the reader the
whole notion of the escape (the rescue of the woman and the Uncle's bachelor-
hood) rests upon an obvious delusion. To understand how this works it is
important to address how the jaunty tone of the story is offset by its setting,
which is in a Gothic world associated with carriages and the ghosts of those who
once rode in them. The Uncle tries to sleep off his intoxication in an old-style
carriage that he discovers amongst some dilapidated mail coaches, described as
'the decaying skeletons of departed mails, and in that lonely place, at that time
of night, they looked chill and dismal' (p. 648). This is a Gothic world of
spectral carriages which takes the Uncle back into a projected past which

---

[17] Marcus, 'Pickwick Revisited', p. 197.

[18] Charles Dickens, *The Pickwick Papers* (Harmondsworth: Penguin, 2003), p. 659. Further
reference to the novel will be inserted parenthetically in the text.

appears real to him so that when he awakens he looks for the woman only to find 'there was neither door nor seat to the coach – it was a mere shell' (p. 659). In the end there is just the skeletal remains of the carriage and 'the ghosts' (p. 659) which inhabit them. The comic tone of the tale works against the Gothic narrative about delusion, ghosts, and the rot of the past and this is what the Uncle has also sworn an allegiance to. The Gothic setting is at odds with its comic tone because within the comedy there lurks this other Gothic tale which is about how the pull of the past, and an allegiance to it, makes it impossible for the Uncle to envisage a future of matrimonial happiness. The tales in *The Pickwick Papers* thus focus on forms of confinement which are either physically, temporally, or emotionally inescapable. One of the key characteristics of this confining Gothic world is repetition.

The 'Nurse's Stories', as Bowen noted, used repetition to generate much of their horror. The form of the tale is delirious and the content is about death, eating people, inexplicable murders, and yet told in the jaunty tones of the nurse so that 'Gothic terror, Gothic laughter, narrative force and diabolic repetition are inextricably and compulsively entwined'.[19] Marcus also notes that the language of *The Pickwick Papers* uses 'repetitive modes' because the interpolated Gothic tales employ a language which is 'encapsulated, stuck, encysted, and embedded in the movement of the novel which moves about and around them'.[20] The freedoms of the novel stand in stark contrast to the restricted, static, worlds developed in the inset tales. These ideas about entrapment repeatedly appear in Dickens around institutions of confinement and in representations of mindsets which suggest an uncanny psychic claustrophobia. As we shall see, his reflections on death-cell states of mind bring these two Gothic narratives together.

This Element does not promise to be the last word on the issue of Dickens' contribution to the Gothic as it is very precisely focused on forms of Gothic confinement which appear either in emotional states or within institutions and does not address wider issues about monstrous characterisations, or the role of the urban Gothic. It argues that the Gothic shapes forms of confinement which hold back the subject by limiting how they perceive the world, thereby denying them the possibility of either personal or social reform. The psychological investigation of this condition also reflects a wider sense of social and political unease. What Dickens suggests is that the Gothic blocks the ability to envisage a way out of social problems and so inhibits any attempt to establish a reformist agenda which must begin by making the type of connections that Gothic confinement, with its pervading form of psychological and social alienation, precludes. As we shall see, *Bleak House* provides a paradigm for moving

---

[19] Bowen, 'Charles Dickens and the Gothic', p. 263.   [20] Marcus, 'Pickwick Revisited', p. 197.

beyond this Gothic blockage as it invites readers to make links that its characters cannot. The novel, for example, indicates that Jo the crossing-sweeper catches smallpox due to the economic neglect of the area where he lives, Tom-all-Alone's, and passes smallpox on to those he comes in contact with when sweeping the road (and also, of course, Esther Summerson). The political mismanagement of an area of London by the interchangeable Lord Coodle, Lord Boodle, and Sir Thomas Doodle, thus creates a disease which spreads beyond its confines so that political neglect has implications for the wider society. The novel's repeated refrain is to ask the reader to think about these connections in order to identify the source of the problem and so generate possible solutions to them. These social problems also have clear psychological consequences and Dickens, in establishing a new way of looking at the world, develops a new version of the Gothic which exists as a precondition for establishing personal and social reform. This study advances an analysis of character psychology by examining how Dickens' contribution explores the emotionally corrosive consequences of the alienation generated by the industrial economy. In Dickens the Gothic is that which must be overcome for reform and personal redemption to occur and this is why Dickens will repeatedly identify the danger which lurks within institutions, mentalities, and even the humour of an inset story such as 'The Story of the Bagman's Uncle'. This study therefore advances a new way of reading these moments of physical and psychological confinement by exploring how the Gothic needs to be moved beyond in order for personal and political freedoms to be fully developed.

Section 1, on 'Prisons', focuses on Dickens' representation of places of incarceration. This is notably clear in his account of prisons which frequently address the psychological effects of incarceration, including accounts of death-cell psychology in his journalism and *Oliver Twist* (1838), and solitary confinement as a mode of self-haunting in the *American Notes* (1842). Dickens extends this idea of self-entrapment and modes of punishment in his account of Bill Sikes' attempt to leave behind Jacob's Island after Nancy's murder only for him to be haunted by projections of her ghost which enforces his return and symbolic execution by the community. The issues of repetition, return, and incarceration are the fundamental Gothic registers explored here. They also play a role in Dickens' representations of law courts, such as Chancery in *Bleak House*, which represent other forms of Gothic entrapment.

Section 2, 'History', explores the return of the past, and characters who are stuck in the past. This is an issue that informs Dickens' views on history and on childhood. Pip in *Great Expectations* attempts to elude the expectations set by his childhood but ultimately finds himself bought by Magwich. Miss Havisham's wedding feast ties her to a past in which she is represented as a skeletal Gothic bride, intent on revenge. Esther Summerson in *Bleak House* tries to make sense of her parentage by a return to a past which makes her the symbolic ghost, heard pacing the terrace at Chesney Wold, haunting the Dedlocks. In *Bleak House*, the legal system is linked to symbolic representations of ghosts and a model of the Female Gothic in which orphaned daughters seek out their mothers. The return to the past is invariably problematic as witnessed by his apocalyptic account of the Gordon Riots in *Barnaby Rudge* (1841) and the abuse of aristocratic authority in *A Tale of Two Cities* (1859), a novel in which noble self-sacrifice thwarts state violence. The section also explores the use of space in *The Old Curiosity Shop* (1841) in which the shop itself provides a jumbled and confused version of history in which characters are symbolically trapped. The past is repeatedly rendered Gothic when it holds people back, literally and symbolically entombs them, and makes it impossible for characters to move on because the past is characterised by misdeeds that need to be revisited. This return to the past, this section argues, is as much psychological as social or political.

Section 3, 'Ghosts', explores the issue of entrapment in Dickens' ghost stories. Dickens asserts a number of ways in which forms of Gothic entrapment can be eluded, but this requires forms of self-reflection that his haunted figures are often initially denied. 'The Signalman' (1866) centres on a repeated confusion about whether ghostly messages have been sent, understood, or are 'real'. The story provides a paradigm for reading the ghost story for its cryptic warnings in which the narrator becomes progressively implicated in a tale that refuses to give up its message in any coherent way. The signalman is trapped in a narrative that he can make little sense of as even the narrator appears to contribute to the confused messages that the signalman, and the reader of the tale, struggle to interpret. The issue of repetition is clear here, as warnings are repeated but misread and there is no escape from the Gothic sense of doom which colours the signalman's plight. The signalman appears as inert, trapped by his inability to act. In *A Christmas Carol* (1843) Scrooge has become inert as his capital and it requires a revisiting of his past and a reflection on his present, before he is able to plot a new future for himself when he overcomes stasis by putting himself back in social circulation and his money into economic circulation. He is shown a version of his future that he does not want to repeat in reality and this enables him to break the chains (and there are many ghosts held back by chains in the narrative) that can only take him into one possible Gothic future. The ghosts need to be left behind for this to happen as Marley gains some form of redemption by stopping Scrooge from repeating his fate. The issue of repetition and forms of psychological and social entrapment also characterise *The Chimes* (1844), *The Haunted Man* (1848), and 'The Hanged Man's Bride'

(1857) and the interpolated stories in *The Pickwick Papers* such as 'The Story of the Goblins Who Stole a Sexton' and 'The Story of the Bagman's Uncle', outlined here.

Dickens' contribution to the Gothic is various; we can see how he generates an urban Gothic in order to address pressing social and political concerns. He also recycles and repositions plot devices and forms of characterisation which have been drawn from an earlier Gothic tradition. While Radcliffe is a clear influence on Dickens it is also important to acknowledge the continuing legacy of Horace Walpole's Gothic. Walpole's *The Castle of Otranto* (1764) inaugurated the idea that the past requires negotiation and appeasement which is a theme that Dickens also addresses. Walpole's novel is also interested in how the past is made present via figures which can supernaturally step out of ancestral portraits, which is, as we shall see, also an idea that Dickens explores in *Bleak House*. However, identifying the precise grounds on which a specifically Dickensian Gothic appears has never been straightforward because in Dickens the Gothic is seemingly everywhere (pervading forms of representation and plot developments) and simultaneously nowhere (because many of these forms are ostensibly comic). It is by focusing directly on forms of confinement that we can begin to see where, and why, Dickens starts to develop a genuinely new form of Gothic writing.

1 Prisons

Sketches by Boz (1836) includes 'A Visit to Newgate' which concludes with Dickens' imaginative contemplation of the likely feelings of a male prisoner in the condemned cell during their final hours. Dickens speculates that they would fall asleep and dream about a possible escape, during which they apologise to their wife for their cruel behaviour, before rushing towards a freedom in which 'the open fields are gained and the broad wide country lies before him'.[21] However, the prisoner wakes in the cell and realises 'He is the condemned felon again, guilty and despairing; and in two hours more will be dead' (p. 210). The essay initiates Dickens' extensive assessments of prisons, prisoners, and regimes of prison discipline that populate his fiction and journalism. In this first exploration of the effects of carceral experience, it is noteworthy that Dickens argues for an elision between institutions and mentalities. His initial description of Newgate refers to it as 'the gloomy depository of the guilt and misery of London' (p. 199). This evocation of a social problem hinges on 'guilt' and who

---

[21] Charles Dickens, 'A Visit to Newgate' in Michael Slater (ed.), *Dickens' Journalism: Sketches by Boz and Other Early Papers 1833–39* (London: Dent, 1996), pp. 199–210, p. 220. Further reference to this item will be inserted parenthetically in the text.

is responsible for it and it becomes reasserted in the later view of the prisoner as 'guilty and despairing'. Social issues thus become psychologically introjected as Dickens addresses the internalisation of a guilty conscience in which the prisoner seeks to make amends with his wife; dreaming that he would 'fall on his knees before her' to 'fervently beseech her pardon for all the unkindness and cruelty that wasted her form and broke her heart!' (p. 210). Notably, his sense of guilt is not related to the undisclosed crime for which he has been found guilty. Guilt thus operates on different levels, it is personal (the domestic narrative about his wife), institutional (he has been found guilty of a crime), and social (the guilty 'gloomy depository' of London life). The relationship between these three expressions of guilt implicates different formations of incarceration – the institutional, the psychological, and the social. How they relate to each depends upon an idea of self-haunting which is rooted within the Gothic.

Prisons appear in a number of Gothic novels and images of the Inquisition can be found in Matthew Lewis' *The Monk* (1796), Ann Radcliffe's *The Italian* (1797), and Charles Maturin's *Melmoth the Wanderer* (1820). Many key scenes of William Godwin's *Caleb Williams* (1794) centre on the injustice of Caleb's incarceration and the manipulation of the law which led to it. Dickens was clearly aware, as exemplified by his comments about Elizabeth Fry and Ann Radcliffe discussed in the Introduction, of how prisons were represented in an earlier Gothic tradition and was trying to find a new Gothic idiom which captured the contemporary experience of incarceration. The psychological effects of imprisonment play a key role in generating the Gothic horrors of this confinement.

How prisons relate to formations of subjectivity and damaged psychological states in Dickens, has been subject to considerable critical discussion. Lionel Trilling's reading of the prison in *Little Dorrit* (1857) argues that the idea of the prison experience becomes incorporated into a range of different theological, social, and psychological formations of the subject, in which the theme of incarceration extends to 'persons and classes being imprisoned by their notions of predestined fate or of religious duty, or by their occupations, their life-schemes, their ideas of themselves, their very habits of language'.[22] For Trilling the key to opening up this internalisation is Freud, because his model of the mind explains the complex patterns of guilt in *Little Dorrit* in which we witness how 'the internal life is in the form, often fantastically parodic, of a criminal process in which the mind is at once the criminal, the victim, the police, the judge, and the executioner'.[23] There will be more to say about the

---

[22] Lionel Trilling, 'Little Dorrit', *The Kenyon Review*, Autumn 1953, Vol. 15, No. 4, 577–90 (p. 579).

[23] Trilling, 'Little Dorrit', p. 581.

Gothic uncanny and its role in this, but it is striking that engagements with Freud
are frequently reasserted in readings of Dickens' prisons and the mentalities
they formulate. Jeremy Tambling, for example, while following a Foucauldian
line on the internalisation of Bentham's Panopticon, as a means of psychologically controlling the prisoner, argues that the Panopticon represents 'the super-
ego' taking control over the rebellious Id of criminal transgression.[24] Sean
Grass, however, has challenged this idea of the internalisation of the
Panopticon in Dickens in part because Bentham's plans were never fully
developed during the period that Dickens was writing, which makes it difficult
to assert its influence on the incarcerated mind of Dickens' felons. He does,
however, acknowledge that a new form of introspective writing is produced in
accounts of prisoners which, as in Dickens' reflections on Newgate, require
a speculative autobiographical construction of the prisoner's experience. Grass'
analysis of this reasserts the importance of guilt in generating these new forms
of subjectivity in which, rather than Panoptic surveillance, 'the exercise of
power ... had to do with locking the self in solitude, inscribing guilt upon it
to account for its own disordered identity and guilty desire, and seizing the
power to subject that self-account to the inventive power of the authorial
other.'[25] Grass notes that Dickens' account of Newgate begins with
a refutation of the statistical evidence that he could have used to support his
reformist agenda because Dickens wanted to address the idea 'that reading the
prison – and narrating it – requires recourse to a concealed psychological world
that facts alone cannot penetrate'.[26] The strategies employed by Dickens to
animate what is a social narrative about crime thus translates guilt into psychological terms, and these are the terms which implicate the presence of a Gothic
uncanniness in which subjects are incarcerated within mental processes which
are governed by repetition. In the uncanny, as in the prison, there is no way out
and this points towards a Gothic formation of subjectivity, characterised by an
inability to escape the forces that have come to haunt it. Dickens' imaginary
prisoner dreams of a possible escape and domestic redemption, but the tragedy
of the piece is that this is precisely imaginary as he finds himself back in the
condemned cell.

Freud's 'The Uncanny' (1919) has played an important role in Gothic
criticism and the model of repetition which defines it is anticipated in
Dickens' version of the psychologically incarcerated self. The repetition

---

[24] Jeremy Tambling, 'Prison-Bound: Dickens and Foucault', *Essays in Criticism*, 1986, Vol. xxxvi,
No. 1, 11–31, (p. 12).
[25] Sean Grass, *The Self in the Cell: Narrating the Victorian Prisoner* (London: Routledge, 2013), p.
29.
[26] Grass, *Self in the Cell*, p. 61.

compulsion and the return of the repressed which characterise the uncanny are also developed into a form of doubling which equally suggests that the subject is incapable of escaping from what are projected versions of themselves. For Freud, the double had once represented a type of protection against death, but once the subject moves beyond narcissistic, and infantile, ideas about immortality the double becomes 'the uncanny harbinger of death', as the subject becomes aware of their finite existence.[27] This double also functions as a type of conscience which psychologically regulates behaviour and so kills off rebellious impulses which become repressed – only to return in moments of uncanniness. These returns are Gothic, in part because 'The "double" has become a thing of terror' as it represents what has been supposedly safely cast off.[28] Images of the dead undead provide, for Freud, clear examples of uncanniness because 'many people experience the feeling in the highest degree in relation to death and dead bodies, to the return of the dead, and to spirits and ghosts'.[29] This has links to the images of self-haunting which populate Dickens' accounts of death-cell psychology, representing a form of psychological entrapment which reflects on the horror of a literal (doubled) physical *and* emotional form of incarceration. In *Oliver Twist* (1838) Fagin's final night in the death cell illustrates this.

Unlike the Newgate prisoner, Fagin has no domestic narrative that he seeks to make amends for. His plight is externalised as we watch him suffer with his realisation that there is no possibility of escape in dreams. Indeed, Fagin is described as 'awake, but dreaming'[30] and is conscious of being haunted by men who had been executed due to his evidence:

> some of them might have inhabited that very cell – sat upon that very spot . . .
> The cell had been built for many years. Scores of men must have passed their
> last hours there. It was like sitting in a vault strewn with dead bodies – the cap,
> the noose, the pinioned arms, the faces that he knew. (p. 469)[31]

The uncanny plays a role in this place which is populated by ghosts in which Fagin is in a ghostly, liminal, awake, and asleep, state as he apprehends these terrifying figures from his past. These spectres also represent figures who are inescapable for Fagin because he implicitly acknowledges his place in a genealogy of crime that links them to him. His journey stands in stark contrast to that of Oliver who is able to transcend a false criminal genealogy that he had

---

[27] Freud, 'The Uncanny', p. 357.   [28] Freud, 'The Uncanny', p. 358.
[29] Freud, 'The Uncanny', p. 364.
[30] Charles Dickens, *Oliver Twist* (Harmondsworth: Penguin, 1985), p. 470. Further reference to this novel will be inserted parenthetically in the text.
[31] I discuss this scene within the context of Dickens' views on capital punishment in *Gothic Death 1740–1914: A Literary History* (Manchester: Manchester University Press, 2016), pp. 113–19.

found himself in as he does not morally or socially belong to it. The one good deed that Fagin can make in the condemned cell is to indicate to Oliver the whereabouts of the papers concerning Oliver's true family history that Monks had given him to store, although this seems like a trade as Fagin in his delirium thinks that Oliver has come to save him. Fagin is beyond redemption whereas Oliver has managed to escape. Genealogies of birth and criminality cross at this point and Fagin is left with his fears of death despite this qualified good deed.

These images of incarceration raise the question of whether reform is possible, when reformation is conceived of as both a social act and a moral possibility. The question is whether good deeds in themselves are sufficient to generate reform, or whether there is a point at which, as for Fagin, the tragedy is that they come too late (and in Fagin's case without obvious sincerity). The plight of Bill Sikes also illustrates this.

Sikes, after murdering Nancy, goes on the run but psychologically he does not get far. He imagines that he is pursued because he is 'haunted' by 'that morning's ghastly figure following at his heels' (p. 428). This is, of course, the figure of Nancy. Sikes' attempts to elude this spectre prove futile:

> At times, he turned, with desperate determination, resolved to beat this phantom off, though it should look him dead; but the hair rose on his head, and his blood stood still, for it had turned with him and was behind him then. He had kept it before him that morning, but it was behind now – always. He leaned his back against a bank and felt that it stood above him, visibly out against the cold night-sky. He threw himself upon the road – on his back upon the road. At his head it stood, silent, erect, and still – a living grave-stone, with its epitaph in blood. (p. 428)

The novel suggests that Sikes cannot escape what he has done and that this pursuit represents the triumph of 'justice' (p. 428). The encounter also suggests both the presence of a conscience and Freud's 'uncanny harbinger of death' as this anticipates the 'corpse endowed with the mere machinery of life' (p. 428), that he is also becoming. Sikes is terrified by this encounter with a corpse-like ghost, and its presence prompts him, unconsciously, to undertake good deeds as a type of amends. He finds himself in the country, and confronted by a house on fire, assists in trying to put it out; in this danger 'he bore a charmed life, and had neither scratch nor bruise, nor weariness nor thought' (p. 430). His honourable efforts do not amount to much because despite them all that is left is 'smoke and blackened ruins' (p. 430). With nowhere to go, and nowhere to hide Sikes returns to London and finds himself shunned by the community of Jacob's Island where he had lived. His attempt to escape the police in a rooftop pursuit involves the use of a rope to help descend a building. The rope, looped under his armpits, slips around his neck as he stumbles when confronted by the gaze of his spectral tormentor, 'The eyes again!' (p. 453), he falls and is hanged.

Sikes cannot escape the spectre, or justice. He is symbolically executed by the community opinion of his once criminal fraternity. He, like Fagin, is beyond redemption. Good deeds, as they occur in the Newgate narrative and the accounts of Fagin and Sikes, come too late. These are also issues in which the Gothic plays a key role in establishing why reform is not possible. Neither Fagin, nor Sikes, can be construed as victims of the system, rather their fates are, the novel suggests, seemingly justified. Self-reform and the possibility of political reform can only be achieved, Dickens argues, by those who can cast off the Gothic narrative which traps them within a world populated by the uncanny dead undead. A counter figure to these Gothic images of physical and psychological incarceration can be found in Mr Pickwick.

It was noted in the Introduction that Steven Marcus has proposed a reading of *The Pickwick Papers* which argues that the freedoms of literary expression that characterise the main plot are challenged by the use of interpolated tales which stress the presence of confinement, in what are often Gothic texts which focus on forms of haunting. Marcus notes of the language used in such tales that 'It tends to be almost uniformly to be obsessed, imprisoned, anal, caught in various immobile, repetitive modes', which Bowen had identified as a feature of Dickens' 'Nurse's Stories'.[32] For Marcus the novel makes a 'momentous turn of development' when Pickwick finds himself incarcerated in the Fleet prison because he refuses to pay costs when he loses his case for breach of promise with Mrs Bardwell.[33]

While in the Fleet, Pickwick makes arrangements to rent a room from one of the other prisoners who is described as a 'Chancery prisoner' (p. 563), which anticipates the forms of legal and fiscal entrapment that Dickens develops in *Bleak House* (1853). The prisoner is described as 'a tall, gaunt, cadaverous man ... with sunken cheeks, and a restless, eager eye. His lips were bloodless, and his bones sharp and thin' (p. 564). The surrender of his room to Pickwick prompts Pickwick to offer the rooms back to him on any occasion in which he would like to meet quietly with his friends. The prisoner indicates that he is friendless because of his time in the prison 'I could not be more forgotten or unheeded than I am here. I am a dead man – dead to society, without the pity they bestow on those whose souls have passed to judgment' (p. 564). Again, prisoners become figures of the uncanny dead undead, and Pickwick's encounters with their stories are designed to make visible, by exteriorising, their plights. The novel focuses on what and whom Pickwick encounters, rather

---

[32] Marcus, 'Pickwick Revisited', p. 197.   [33] Marcus, 'Pickwick Revisited', p. 200.

than elaborating from within the type of death-cell psychology that Dickens employs elsewhere. Pickwick meets Alfred Jingle, an actor he had once known, who possesses a verbally eccentric line in narrative précis. Jingle has pawned most of his clothes and summarises his likely plight as 'Nothing soon – lie in bed – starve – die – Inquest – little bone-house – poor prisoner – common necessaries – hush it up – gentlemen of the jury – warden's tradesmen – keep it snug – natural death – coroner's order – workhouse funeral – serve him right – all over – drop the curtain' (p. 568). Pickwick helps to bail Jingle out so that he avoids this plight.

The scenes in the prison serve as a way of enlightening Pickwick about the dead undead lives of its inhabitants and the likely scenarios in which their lives are likely to end. Grass evidences some critical frustration with the novel because it 'denies us more than oblique and momentary access to the private world of the self in the cell', leading him to conclude that this is an omission caused by Dickens' own familial experience of the Marshalsea debtor's prison in which his father spent some time.[34] Marcus, however, proposes an alternative reading of Pickwick's experiences which, implicitly, suggests that a reformist attitude becomes possible by moving beyond a Gothic language centred on incarceration and repetition – a possibility denied in the representations of Dickens' death-cell Newgate prisoner and the plights of Fagin and Sikes.

At one level Pickwick seems to have become absorbed by the narratives of imprisonment which permeates the language of the law. Marcus notes that this language of the law reflects on both Pickwick's incarceration and on Dickens' imaginative ambitions for the novel. As Pickwick is:

> confined within the world or precincts of the law, Dickens' writing too becomes imprisoned and immobile, preoccupied again as it was in the tales with intensities and obsessions and closeness and deprivation and filth, bound in by the law, by cases, by the past, by the accumulated weight of mold and dirt and misery that the prison and the law represent.[35]

The interpolated tales are about incarceration (among the Gothic tales are also two, 'The Old Man's Tale and the Queer Client' and 'The Story of the Convict's Return', which directly reflect on the consequences of imprisonment), and Pickwick now seems to have entered into this circumscribed world. The exteriority noted above, however, moves these prison stories into a different realm because they invite forms of critical contemplation which are different in kind to those prompted by Gothic images of incarceration. As Marcus notes, the account of Pickwick's prison experiences is 'not exactly the

---

[34] Grass, *Self in the Cell*, pp. 64, 65.   [35] Marcus, 'Pickwick Revisited', p. 200.

same as the writing in the interpolated tales' because the representation of the encounters in the Fleet 'is harder and has a greater bite to it'.[36] This is because Dickens' reformist agenda comes through in this account, as witnessed by how a number of social issues become implicated as responsible for the fated, dead undead, life of the prisoner. The freedoms of the imagination which Marcus sees as characterising the main narrative become challenged by engagement with social reform which suggests that social and economic freedoms constitute realities which exist beyond Dickens' linguistic play. For Marcus 'writing, which before was free, has become like Mr. Pickwick himself engaged and involved, and engaged and involved with society', so that beneath the often comedic play of language there appears this other, socially committed engagement, which moves beyond both comedy and the Gothic forms of entrapment because 'Property and money are more than words, and words cannot make you free of them'.[37] Words thus take you back to the material context which they may attempt to evade. Dickens is here looking for a way out of these forms of Gothic incarceration and the awakening of a reformist mindset, which is aware of material reality, provides that possibility. This idea of social and economic reform also informs his interest in political regimes which are different from those found in Britain. His account of America illuminates what happens when reformist optimism becomes progressively undermined, which leads Dickens back into a contemplation of a Gothic uncanny and the psychology of incarceration.

Dickens' *American Notes for General Circulation* (1842) charts his growing sense of disillusion with America's model of democracy.[38] The travelogue starts with the jaunty optimism of his arrival in Boston, but concludes with his condemnation of slavery as America fails the ultimate test of its own democratic principles. Dickens visited a number of institutions while in America, including prisons, and the narrative pivots on his account of the Eastern Penitentiary in Philadelphia. Dickens deplores the prison's system of solitary confinement which ensures that an inmate is isolated from all social contact, other than with the warders. For Dickens this constitutes a notably cruel form of seclusion which, as in his earlier accounts of incarceration, resembles a dead undead state 'He is a man buried alive; to be dug out in the slow round of years; and in the mean time dead to everything but torturing anxieties and horrible despair'.[39]

---

[36] Marcus, 'Pickwick Revisited', p. 200.   [37] Marcus, 'Pickwick Revisited', p. 200.

[38] I discuss in depth the issue of Dickens' account of spectrality in the *American Notes* in 'Colonial Ghosts: Mimicking Dickens in America' in Avril Horner and Sue Zlosnik (eds.), *Le Gothic* (Basingstoke: Palgrave, 2008), pp. 185–200.

[39] Charles Dickens, *The American Notes for General Circulation* (Harmondsworth: Penguin, 1985), p. 148. Further reference to this text will be inserted parenthetically in the text.

The prisoner becomes a non-person, even the officer who delivers his meals is unaware of the prisoner's name, crime, and length of sentence. He is identified merely by a number over his cell door and is unaware of which part of the prison he is held in. Dickens' portraits of the prisoners reflect this mournful existence with one prisoner whose bed 'looked by-the-by like a grave' (p. 150). He notes of another he looked 'as wan and unhealthy as if he had been summoned from his grave' (p. 150). As Dickens proceeds through the prison he begins the process of imaginatively inhabiting their plights. He imagines that the attempt to populate the cells on either side simply generates faceless figures which 'have a mystery that makes him [the prisoner] tremble' (p. 154). The prisoner's fears take on a spectral form when they generate a figure that comes to occupy the corner of his cell which becomes 'every night the lurking-place of a ghost: a shadow: – a silent something' (p. 155), which begins to haunt him in an inescapable way so that he dreads having to return to his cell after his daily exercise because 'When night comes, there stands the phantom in the corner. If he has the courage to stand in its place, and drive it out (he had once: being desperate), it broods upon his bed' (p. 155). This is the experience of the living dead that we have seen in Dickens' account of life in the condemned cell. Here the experience is made a perpetual living death in which all identity becomes expunged with Dickens recording that 'In every little chamber that I entered, and at every grate through which I looked, I seemed to see the same appalling countenance' (p. 156), in an experience which 'makes the senses dull' (p. 157), as the prisoners are progressively depersonalised as they become incrementally erased. For Grass, in this instance we witness a delirious assimilation of Foucault's idea of panoptic surveillance in which a prisoner becomes self-haunted by an internalisation of a gaze that manifests as that ghost in the corner of the cell.[40] For Grass, Dickens' focus on the psychology of the death cell transforms 'the prison novel from the inquiry into social justice it had been during the eighteenth century into the eminently internal, psychological narrative that we recognise today as a modern understanding of the effects of the cell'.[41] This, however, is only part of the picture and one which appears only within the Gothic narratives which focus on the uncanny prisoner who is, crucially, beyond redemption. In effect, two versions of the prison are addressed by Dickens, one in which (as in *The Pickwick Papers*), the system itself is placed under social scrutiny, with the intention of flagging the importance of reform, and the other which focuses on the psychological consequences of forms of incarceration and criminals (such as Fagin and Sikes), who are beyond redemption if not, in Fagin's case, beyond pity. These positions become blurred

---

[40] Grass, *Self in the Cell*, p. 78.   [41] Grass, *Self in the Cell*, p. 78.

when taking into account the plight of the prisoner in solitary confinement because there the analysis condemns a regime because of the psychological suffering that it produces. To a degree, this is a more nuanced position and it indicates how the Gothic narrative, centring on living dead 'ghosts', can be challenged by a reformist narrative that parades the ghost in order to critique the system.

Prisons clearly constitute a way for Dickens to think about how socially reformist issues can be presented and he uses prisons in a similar fashion in *Little Dorrit* and *A Tale of Two Cities*, where they play a key role in establishing how the past comes to bear on the present, a process which will be discussed at length in the following section. The representations of self-haunting that we witness in the death cell, or in forms of solitary confinement, rely on models of ghosting which also bear an imprint of the spectre that we find in the more formal ghost stories, which are discussed in Section 3. It is also noteworthy that Dickens elides places of incarceration with systems (such as the law) which also incarcerate the subject. These systems too are often imbued with a Gothic presence which provides a check on Dickens' social reformist agenda. The role of the law, so central to these prison narratives, plays a key role in this and becomes an institution which is subject to sustained critical scrutiny in *Bleak House*, a novel which invites a consideration of how law, politics, and economics represent modes of entrapment.

Robert Mighall has argued that *Bleak House* is 'Dickens's most all-embracing social critique' and 'his most consummate and sustained Gothic performance'.[42] Chancery is the key institution here as it consumes the time, money, and lives of those who are caught up in its suits, with all of the characters to some degree pulled into its world. For Mighall, Chancery functions like a version of the Inquisition that we find in the writings of Charles Maturin and Edgar Allan Poe, it is 'implacable in its heartless indifference to suffering, and sinister in the tortuous "mysteries" only its initiates can understand'.[43] Chancery represents a pernicious social problem which generates 'Fog everywhere' as it conceals its vested interests by disguising them as legitimate, because resolvable, legal cases.[44] It is noted that 'at the very heart of the fog sits the Lord High Chancellor in his High Court of Chancery' (p. 50). While the novel uses the case of Jarndyce and Jarndyce to pull in the central characters, Dickens also widens the scope of legal malpractice to include characters such as Jo the Crossing Sweeper and Krook, the keeper of texts that he cannot read. The novel has clear Gothic engagements which can also be gendered as noted by Alison Milbank (1992), who has explored how Dickens draws upon an earlier

---

[42] Mighall, 'Dickens and the Gothic', p. 86.   [43] Mighall, 'Dickens and the Gothic', p. 87.
[44] Charles Dickens, *Bleak House* (Harmondsworth: Penguin, 1985), p. 49. Further reference to this novel will be inserted parenthetically in the text.

Female Gothic tradition associated with Ann Radcliffe, to represent the feelings of loss and entrapment variously suffered by Esther and Lady Dedlock. It is, however, the controlling metaphor of the fog and the blindness that it generates which provides links to images of entrapment which have characterised the prison writings, and it is here that the Gothic plays a significant role in shaping models of alienation.

In representations of the death cell, recanting comes too late and the figures are beyond redemption. In *The Pickwick Papers* Pickwick can eventually come out of prison and his journey within it is used to highlight the failings of the judiciary (in its widest sense, but also to include forms of incarceration). He steps out of an ostensible Gothic narrative because he is not trapped within the type of Gothic tale that, Marcus has noted, characterise many of the interpolated tales. For Marcus, this is because Pickwick's prison scenes are intended to create connections which 'represent society and its structures, in particular, those structures known as property and money'.[45] The social reformist agenda becomes possible because of this ability to step outside of the Gothic space of the prison and to reflect on how social and economic issues influence legal judgments. The invitation to the reader is to make these connections in order to conceive of a different, putatively politically radical, way of contemplating the legal process rather than to reflect on the self-destructive plights of Sikes and Fagin. How to connect these issues is central to the detective narrative in *Bleak House*, which implicates Lady Dedlock in an affair which illustrates how the repressed elements of the past continue to haunt the present. Those who are victims of the system, such as Jo, invite a contemplation of how their plight can be attributed to the abuse of social and economic power. To make these links is to move beyond the Gothic as it requires a clarity of thought which Chancery's fog attempts to baffle. The novel pauses to reflect on the places, peoples and products that seemingly constitute the capacious range of the social world that the novel contemplates:

> What connexion can there be, between the place in Lincolnshire, the house in town, the Mercury in powder, and the whereabouts of Jo the outlaw with the broom, who had that distant ray of light upon him when he swept the church-yard-step? What connexion can there have been between so many people in the innumerable histories of this world, who, from opposite sides of great gulfs, have, nevertheless, been very curiously brought together! (p. 272)

The scale of connection that the reader is invited to contemplate reflects on the ambitions of the detective narrative in which Inspector Bucket's investigation into Tulkinghorn's murder leads to the exposure of Lady Dedlock's affair with

---

[45] Marcus, 'Pickwick Revisited', p. 200.

Captain Hawdon. In the above passage, a series of seemingly unrelated issues are set out as clues. By linking them the social reformist ambition of the novel, which is to move beyond the confines of forms of Gothic entrapment, becomes clear.

Tom-all-Alone's has, as its name suggests, been abandoned and is caught-up in a Chancery suit which beggars everyone. The place 'is a black, dilapidated street, avoided by all decent people' whose 'tumbling tenements contain, by night, a swarm of misery' (p. 272). This 'swarm' is the pestilence which is generated out of this neglect in which 'these ruined shelters have bred a crowd of foul existence that crawls in and out of gaps . . . in maggot numbers, where the rain drips in . . . fetching and carrying fever' (pp. 272–73). Jo is incapable of making the connections that the preceding scene invites because, the novel asserts, of his illiteracy. Jo is unable to read the characters and symbols of shop signs and is also estranged from the process of handling documents which is so central to the activities of Chancery. Jo's plight is summarised as a tragic one, 'To see people read, and to see people write, and to see the postman deliver letters, and not to have the least idea of all that language – to be, to every scrap of it, stone blind and dumb!' (p. 274). The links between Chancery and Tom-all-Alone's also implicate Chancery's role in generating a 'blindness' which makes it difficult for connections to be made. These are connections which enable an escape from the Gothic confines of the Chancery suits whereas Jo is construed as a victim of the system, forced to inhabit a pestilential urban Gothic slum. Crucially, however, the fever induced by the slum cannot be contained by the place that produces it, 'he has his revenge. Even the winds are his messengers, and they serve him in these hours of darkness. There is not a drop of Tom's corrupted blood but propagates infection and contagion somewhere' (p. 683). This revenge is against the society whose neglect has created the pestilential conditions of the area, this fever 'shall work its retribution, through every order of society, up to the proudest of the proud, and to the highest of the high' (p. 683), as Dickens charts the idea of a self-destructive society whose destruction had been caused by an inability to acknowledge the interdependent worlds articulated in that invitation to connect. *Bleak House* focuses on the law as a type of corrupting presence, Dickens returned to these issues in *Little Dorrit* (1857).

The psychological and emotional effects of incarceration are central to *Little Dorrit* which explores a number of institutions, including the Marshalsea, which shapes the lives of the Dorrit family even after William Dorrit, an inmate in the prison for over twenty years, is released. His daughter Amy (or Little Dorrit) is born in the prison and finds its presence impossible to cast off. When the Dorrits come into money and are able to pay off their debts their attempts to

leave behind the prison's influence while touring the continent represents
a struggle for Amy. While her father wants to pose as a gentleman and deny
his past, Amy sees the prison everywhere. She sees Italy as unreal as a dream,
travelling through a picturesque landscape in a carriage she expects that the
carriage might at any moment 'bring up with a jolt at the old Marshalsea gate'.[46]
The scenes through which they travel 'resembled the unreality of her own inner
life' (p. 488) as she fails to cast off the introjected reality of her prison
experiences. For her, there is the impossibility of eluding 'the well-known
shadow of the Marshalsea wall' (p. 501). William is disturbed by this 'I am
hurt that she should – ha – systematically reproduce what the rest of us blot out'
(p. 503), as he seeks to leave behind and conceal their associations with the
prison. Even the beauty of Venice is haunted by the prison when it is noted that
'It appeared on the whole, to Little Dorrit herself, that this same society in which
they lived, greatly resembled a superior sort of Marshalsea' (p. 536), as it is
populated by characters who 'seemed to come abroad, pretty much as people
had come into prison; through debt, through idleness, relationship, curiosity,
and general unfitness for getting on' (p. 536). Later, on a trip to Rome 'The ruins
of the vast old Amphitheatre, of the old Temples, of the old commemorative
Arches, of the old trodden highways, of the old tombs, besides being what they
were, to her, were ruins of the old Marshalsea' (p. 639). For Amy it has become
a place of uncomfortable self-reflection in which she sees the 'ruins of her own
old life – ruins of the faces and forms that of old people it – ruins of its loves,
hopes, cares, and joys' (p. 639). All of these moments testify to the fact that
Amy is still imaginatively incarcerated within the Marshalsea. It is a plight that
William also shares despite his best efforts to cast off the experience. His speech
at a dinner attended by Italian nobility begins 'Ladies and gentlemen, the duty –
ha – devolves upon me of – hum, welcoming you to the Marshalsea. Welcome to
the Marshalsea! The space is – ha – limited – limited' (pp. 676–78). This is the
start of a mental and physical collapse in which from this moment he 'knew of
nothing beyond the Marshalsea' (p. 679) and subsequently dies.

For Tambling, Dickens' prisons influence 'structures of thought' and generate a version of Blake's 'mind forg'd manacles' that characters struggle to
escape.[47] Mighall notes that with William Dorrit we witness how 'The sphere
of haunting is now confined to the mind'.[48] It is the causes of literal and
imaginative confinement which can be attributed to the presence of the Gothic
which also permeates places and mentalities to suggest that even comparative
innocents, such as William and Amy, struggle to escape from the system. This is

---

[46] Charles Dickens, *Little Dorrit* (Harmondsworth: Penguin, 2003), p. 488. Further reference to this
novel will be inserted parenthetically in the text.
[47] Tambling, 'Dickens and Foucault', p. 11.   [48] Mighall, 'Dickens and the Gothic', p. 91.

suggested in the novel's representation of the prison at Marseilles in which 'A prison taint was on every thing there. The imprisoned air, the imprisoned light, the imprisoned damps, the imprisoned men, were all deteriorated by confinement' (p. 16). The prison in Marseilles is much bleaker than the Marshalsea, but the consequences of prison conditions there are representative of the reach of confinement that also applies to William and Amy. Amy is, ultimately, able to transcend the imaginative confines of imprisonment when she marries Arthur Clennam on his release from prison as the novel moves away from images of Gothic confinement to engage with positive images of redemption generated within the romance plot.

This section has explored how prisons function in physical, social, and psychological contexts. Places of incarceration evoke Gothic mentalities dogged by pasts which have caught up with them. The prison is as much an idea as a real, physical, entity. The Gothic becomes an overdetermined form in these moments in which Gothic spaces produce Gothic mindsets which suggest that what is genuinely horrifying is the inability to envisage a future free of the forces of social and psychological oppression. These spaces also demonstrate how the past catches up with subjects unless they can find a way of casting off those histories. History and its relationship to forms of confinement is the principal focus of the following section which explores how the past, often associated with secrets about identity, returns as a form of the Gothic uncanny. Ancestral secrets trap people in the present. As with William Dorrit, the past is not so easy to cast off and, as so frequently in Dickens, the return of the repressed constitutes another moment in which the Gothic is employed to demonstrate the power of social, psychological and emotional forms of entrapment.

2 History

Towards the end of the previous section there was an account of how William Dorrit, in the end, cannot cast off the influence of the Marshalsea. His tale of entrapment is not the only one in *Little Dorrit*, which also explores the circumstances which culminate in the imprisonment of Arthur Clennam. Arthur is also imprisoned in the Marshalsea, after being unable to pay off the debts incurred by a misguided financial speculation. Arthur, however, is haunted by a different narrative relating to the true identity of his biological mother, even though he had assumed that his stepmother was his true mother. A bequest means that Amy Dorrit becomes aware of this history which Mrs Clennam, shortly before her death, admits to. The documents that would have identified Arthur's true mother are destroyed at Amy's request because she does not want Arthur, with whom she is in love, to have his memories of his supposed mother tarnished. By doing so Amy loses the bequest, but Arthur is restored to wealth and bailed out of the Marshalsea by Doyce, a former business partner. Arthur and Amy marry and the truth of Arthur's parentage is concealed from him. Arthur's story is about success, in love, friendship, and business. His life, however, is potentially dogged by this secret narrative about his real mother's identity, which would, for Arthur, unsettle this. The suppression of that narrative is concealed and enables him to escape the forms of entrapment which have blighted, in a Gothic way, the life of William Dorrit, and indeed Amy, until her marriage with Arthur which also represents a casting off of the gloom of the Marshalsea. As Mighall notes 'It is by forgetting the past that both Arthur and his new bride can escape from the prison house of memory'.[49] Casting off the past and leaving prison are thus closely paralleled in the novel and this illustrates how the continuing presence of the past functions as another mode of entrapment, unless it becomes possible to either escape it or bury it. As in keeping with the representations of the prison as literal and psychological dungeons, this formulation of the past in Dickens is repeatedly associated with the Gothic. For Gill Ballinger 'The Clennam household is ... like an old Gothic castle containing secrets that need to be expunged'.[50] The idea that history might be repeated superficially glosses the idea of an uncanny entrapment which Freud saw in an unabreacted return of the repressed. In this instance, however, the past does not uncannily return and so Gothic forms of entrapment are sidestepped rather than worked through. Some secrets can remain buried and their repression does no lasting damage.

Prisons will be briefly returned to at the end of this section, but it is important to note that prisons and the history that they represent also need to be considered because these are prisons which have often come to the end of their institutional life. Closed prisons and their histories represent another way of engaging with a Gothic past. A recent article on Dickens' prisons notes that for all Dickens' fascination with forms of prison regimes, his focus in the novels is fundamentally retrospective.[51] In 1842 both the Fleet and the Marshalsea were closed. The new prison regime inaugurated in Dickens' working life was the system known as the 'separate system' which required prisoners to be separated to encourage self-reflection on their crimes and 'The modern carceral system

---

[49] Mighall, *Victorian Gothic Fiction*, p. 110.

[50] Gill Ballinger, 'Haunting the Law: Aspects of Gothic in Dickens's Fiction', *Gothic Studies*, 2008, Vol. 10, No. 2, 35–50 (p. 41).

[51] Eleanor March, Dominique Moran, Matt Houlbrook, Yvonne Jukes and Michaela Mahlberg., 'Defining the Carceral Characteristics of the "Dickensian Prison": A Corpus Stylistics Analysis of Dickens's Novels', *Victoriographies*, 2023, Vol. 13, No. 1, 15–41 (p. 22).

required modern prison buildings' which resulted in Pentonville which opened in 1842 which provided the model on which new prisons would be constructed and old ones repurposed.[52] According to Grass 'Dickens never seems to have visited Pentonville' although it is seemingly parodied in *David Copperfield* (1850).[53] Dickens' fiction (as distinct from *The American Notes*) thus focuses on prisons which were 'already historic and obsolete carceral sites'.[54] History itself is thus implicated as a form of imprisonment because these 'obsolete' prisons symbolically reflect on the idea of being imprisoned within history.

This section focuses on the relationship between personal and public histories. It explores how images of doubling and forms of repetition constitute moments where the subject becomes constrained by the past. How to move beyond these constraints involves a casting off of the Gothic. It is also important to note that reflections on the past are not always grounded in Gothic terms. The reflections on personal history that we witness in *Nicholas Nickleby* (1839), *David Copperfield* (1850), and *Great Expectations* (1861), for example, are not obviously conventionally Gothic, whereas the parental history of Esther Summerson in *Bleak House* raises questions about class, gender, and illicit relationships which do have a clear, explicit, Gothic resonance to them. Pip in *Great Expectations* provides a tragicomic reflection in the form of the Bildungsroman, but it also incorporates Gothic elements when the novel reflects on those who have been able to move through history and those who, like Miss Havisham, are seemingly stuck in the past. Pip records his first sight of Miss Havisham:

> I saw that everything within my view which ought to be white, had been white long ago, and had lost its lustre, and was faded and yellow. I saw that the bride within the bridal dress had withered like the dress, and like the flowers, and had no brightness left but the brightness of her sunken eyes.[55]

Havisham's world is characterised by rot. The past has destroyed the present, because her attempt to hold on to a decayed present becomes a reminder of all that she has lost, and cannot move on from. Havisham's world of Gothic decay is a consequence of trying to arrest time which stands in contrast to Pip's forward movement towards a future from which he reflects on the past and what he has learnt from it. This, however, is not without qualification which is registered in Pip's horrified discovery that Magwich is his benefactor, which

---

[52] March, et al., 'Carceral Characteristics', p. 22.   [53] Grass, *Self in the Cell*, p. 51.

[54] March, et al., 'Carceral Characteristics', p. 24.

[55] Charles Dickens, *Great Expectations* (Harmondsworth: Penguin, 1982), p. 87. Further reference to this novel will be inserted parenthetically in the text.

prompts a reference to *Frankenstein*, 'The imaginary student pursued by the misshapen creature he had impiously made, was not more wretched than I, pursued by the creature who had made me, and recoiling from him with a stronger repulsion, the more he admired me and the fonder he was of me' (p. 354). If Arthur Clennam's parentage is concealed from him, which enables him to escape from the past, Pip's symbolic parenting is evoked here. Pip can seemingly more readily accept the Gothic Miss Havisham in this role than Magwich because at this point Pip cannot help but regard Magwich as an illegitimate, and strictly illegal, presence both within Britain and Pip's lodgings. *Frankenstein* is also indebted to the form of the bildungsroman and this moment provides a reflection on that in which Pip imagines himself not as the created, but as the creator, which given the issue of the sponsorship of Pip's great expectations appears to reverse the dynamic of ownership. Pip culturally performs for Magwich, including a recitation in a foreign language, as if Magwich is evaluating his investment. The reference to Mary Shelley's novel suggests that it is Pip who has conjured Magwich and this reversal evokes the language of pursuit and entrapment which is more closely associated with the persecuted Victor Frankenstein than with his creation. The moment also suggests a desire to be self-fashioning that is thwarted by a language of creation and ownership. The confusion of attribution (is Pip the creator, or the created?) illustrates how the subject's autonomy is compromised by the return of the past represented by Magwich. Magwich is, for the child Pip who encounters him at the start of the novel, a type of Gothic ghoul who threatens to eat him and his later return, distilled through Shelley's novel, indicates that this is a return which threatens the idea of agency. Miss Havisham's fashioning of Estella as a creature to carry out her revenge, 'I stole her heart away and put ice in its place' (p. 412), also evokes *Frankenstein* and its narrative concerning symbolic parenting. Knowing where you come from might seem to resolve this, but as Pip's plight suggests, this evokes other Gothic narratives which Arthur in *Little Dorrit* was able to resolve. The same cannot be said of Esther Summerson in *Bleak House*.

Alison Milbank has noted how *Bleak House* draws upon an earlier Radcliffean Female Gothic tradition in its depiction of Esther Summerson. In part, this can be attributed to Esther's secret parentage when it is revealed that she is the illegitimate daughter of Lady Dedlock and Esther's presence in the novel is conflated with older ancestral histories relating to the Dedlocks. The terrace of Chesney Wold, the home of Lord and Lady Dedlock, is seemingly haunted by the ghost of a Lady Dedlock from the time of the Civil War. The novel recounts that the earlier Lord and Lady Dedlock took different sides during the rebellion against Charles I. This republican Lady Dedlock was killed in an accident when she went to lame the horses that her husband and his friends had intended to ride in the fight for the king. Civil war and the tensions within the marriage of the current Lord and Lady Dedlock are elided as the past gains an insistent presence which the Dedlocks' housekeeper, Mrs Rouncewell, notes is reflected in this ghost story which '*must be heard* … You cannot shut it out' (p. 41, italics in original) because the ghost can so often be heard walking on the terrace.

National histories and personal histories become linked when Esther realises that she is Lady Dedlock's illegitimate daughter. Esther, aware of the ghost story, walks on the terrace and reflects 'that there was a dreadful truth in the legend of the Ghost's Walk; that it was I, who was to bring calamity upon the stately house; and that my warning feet were haunting it even then' (p. 571). The revelation that Esther is Lady Dedlock's illegitimate, pre-marital, child threatens to overthrow the aristocratic authority of the Dedlocks, just as the earlier republican Lady Dedlock had threatened the aristocracy with her anti-monarchal sentiments. Esther functions as Lady Dedlock's inescapable uncanny double which threateningly haunts Lady Dedlock's world. For Esther, this identification is a horrifying moment as it enables her to make a number of connections that, as we saw in the discussion of Jo, the novel invites the reader to make. Milbank notes that this realisation prompts Esther to 'flee in terror at the realisation that it is she who is its [Chesney Wold's] ghost, its alienated past, just as she is the embodiment of the absent Bleak House'.[56] Esther at this point resembles the entrapped heroines of the Female Gothic and this issue of entrapment by the past is also shared with Lady Dedlock. The presence of this secret entraps and does so in a Gothic manner because the law, in the guise of Tulkinghorn, intrudes into this secret history as he realises the power that this secret gives him over Lady Dedlock.

Secrets which are kept secret, as in *Little Dorrit*, keep the Gothic at bay. When a secret becomes exposed it traps those who are caught up in it as it ensnares them in histories that they are unable to cast off. Lady Dedlock dies, whereas Arthur Clennam marries and becomes wealthy. Their different journeys can in part be attributed to the class backgrounds with which they are associated. Clennam is forward-looking and progressive whereas the Dedlocks are, as their name not so subtly suggests, locked into the past. Clennam also has much in common with the 'illegitimate' Esther Summerson and like her he is protected from the ramifications of the past. Clennam does not inherit the type of guilty feeling associated with Lady Dedlock, which Gothically ties her to the past.

History and its discontents can be seen in Chesney Wold which is inhabited by its ancestral dead. In a chapter ('National and Domestic'), which charts how

---

[56] Alison Milbank, *Daughters of the House: Modes of Gothic in Victorian Fiction* (Basingstoke: Macmillan, 1992), p. 94.

the setting sun casts shadows over a room containing the portraits of the
Dedlocks, the dead Dedlocks are granted a spectral presence. The fading light
flickers across the faces so that 'Strange movements come upon their
features ... A dense Justice in a corner is beguiled into a wink. A staring
Baronet, with a truncheon, gets a dimple in his chin' (p. 620). The Walpolean
Gothic, with its animated ancestral portrait in *The Castle of Otranto* (1764) is
gestured to here, but these are spectres who wink rather than sigh. These figures
from the past are granted the illusion of life until the sun sets and the moon casts
a more funereal gloom, 'Now, the moon is high; and the great house, needing
habitation more than ever, is like a body without life. Now, it is even awful,
stealing through it, to think of the live people who have slept in the solitary
bedrooms; to say nothing of the dead' (p. 621). The place becomes animated in
a different way. Gone are the winks and the dimples which become replaced by
Gothic images of 'threatening hands raised up' (p. 621) which indicate the
presence of a more menacing, insistent, Walpolean world associated with the
Dedlocks.

For Mighall, Chesney Wold 'is an anachronism; its horrors derive from its
obsolescence and its isolation from the modern world'.[57] This is, however,
a Gothic world which is linked to the pestilential horrors of Tom-all-Alone's
because:

> The unsanitary horrors and physiological taint of the slum has its political
> origins in the Gothic mansion. Thus the smell and taste of the ancient
> Dedlocks in their graves which permeates the estate of Chesney Wold, is
> the smell of a feudal past which appeals to precedent, custom, and ancestry.[58]

Mighall notes that Dickens' view of history was a fundamentally Whiggish one,
characterised by the development and support of 'progressive values'.[59] The
Dedlocks represent the dead hand of history (as Adam Smith might have it),
which holds back reform – a check represented by the miasma which engulfs
Tom-all-Alone's. These symbolic connections require acts of identification and
decoding (as in Esther's identification with the ghost at Chesney Wold). *Bleak
House* emphasises the importance of forms of reading and interpretation and
those who are unable to read, such as Jo and Krook, are left estranged and
disempowered. Their respective narratives resemble the interpolated Gothic
tales in *The Pickwick Papers*, which require specific types of decoding.
Different textual forms (such as the Gothic) and the plights of particular
characters (such as Jo and Krook) invite specific interpretive practices. The
goal is to see through the fog that permeates the novel which obscures the

---

[57] Mighall, *Victorian Gothic Fiction*, p. 70.   [58] Mighall, *Victorian Gothic Fiction*, pp. 74–75.
[59] Mighall, *Victorian Gothic Fiction*, p. 75.

significance of these narratives and blurs the connections between them. To connect enables a reflection on the past and the present which permits characters to transcend the historical forces that constrain them. Inspector Bucket is a key figure as his ability to detect, read, and interpret articulates the novel's wider ambition to foster a reformist agenda which requires the system to be seen in a new, because connected, way. His investigation into Tulkinghorn's murder stands as an exemplary method for decoding the past in order to move into the present. This is an approach, however, which also needs to be applied to Lady Dedlock whose secret affair with Captain Hawdon leads to her exposure and death. This is, arguably, the great secret of the novel and one which demonstrates that the past can kill because you cannot escape it. The task for Esther, as Mighall sees it, is to evade 'the effects of malign legacy' as far as that legacy is associated with the ancestral curse carried by Lady Dedlock.[60] These historical burdens identified by Mighall are also psychological ones and this slippage between history and subjectivity is also important to consider because it demonstrates how ideas about entrapment are manifested as mindsets. As we saw in the previous section, prisons are not just literal entities they are also states of mind which demonstrate how far Dickens is establishing a Gothic psychology – one which is also reflected in how Esther negotiates her position in a narrative centring on Gothic inheritance. The revelation about Esther's parentage is symbolically projected on to Esther who, as we saw earlier, sees herself as *the* secret. The focus therefore concerns the effects of the past on her as she finds herself in a predicament which resembles Arthur Clennam's before Amy's intervention, and this raises issues about the dual narrative structure of *Bleak House.*

The chapters consist of Esther's reflections on her past and a third-person narrator whose texts are in the present tense. The very structure of the novel thus addresses the relationship between the past and the present, but these narratives are not separate, an issue made clear by how Esther reflects on her past in order to address her new, and present, circumstances (which are also retrospectively produced). In order for this to take place there needs to be two Esther Summersons in the text, a position which is acknowledged by the Esther who narrates.

Esther's smallpox leaves lasting marks on her face and her life is effectively demarcated between her pre- and post-smallpox life. On recovery from the illness Esther looks at herself in a mirror:

> I put my hair aside, and looked at the reflection in the mirror, encouraged by seeing how placidly it looked at me. I was very much changed – O very, very

---

[60] Mighall, *Victorian Gothic Fiction*, p. 104.

> much. At first, my face was so strange to me, that I think I should have put my hands before it and started back, but for the encouragement I have mentioned. (p. 559)

This breakdown in the 'I' in this moment of self-reflection represents a turning point in the narrative, albeit one that also reflects on what has been concealed in the narrative structure of the novel up to this point. Cynthia N. Malone summarises:

> The illness that scars Esther's face creates a visible sign of this division within the 'I'; the new, scarred Esther, the fictive narrator, begins her story looking back at the old, beautiful Esther. This event in the plot metaphorically represents the distinction that is always implied in the stance of retrospection, the distinction between an old self and a new self, a narrated 'I' and a narrating 'I'.[61]

The 'I' is therefore unstable in the text, despite the emphasis placed on the revelation of identity. It points to how this new version of Esther uses this doubleness to reflect on what the present means to her. She can see the past in the mirror, but her inner world moves on from this and actively resists attempts to pull her back into the past. This becomes clear in her response to the proposal letter sent by Jarndyce.

Esther is moved by the proposal 'I was very happy, very thankful, very hopeful; but I cried very much' (p. 668). The tears offer a pause for a confused reflection; she looks at herself in the mirror, 'My eyes were red and swollen, and I said, "O Esther, Esther, can that be you!" I am afraid that the face in the glass was going to cry again at this reproach, but I held up my finger at it and it stopped' (p. 668). Malone notes that a scene like this indicates that Esther is now an observer of herself because she can stand outside of herself.[62] This is the point at which a form of agency appears because Esther is prompted to scrutinise the cause of her tears. At this stage she admonishes that weeping version of herself and accepts the proposal, only to be later freed from it to marry Allan Woodcourt. Esther's movements, and the self-reflections which accompany them, progressively move her away from the world of Lady Dedlock. Jarndyce was her guardian and although a kindly figure, is symbolically Esther's surrogate father. In this way, Esther is ultimately able to move away from the past by casting off these parental figures. History in *Bleak House* is political, feudal, and personal. It is familial and as in the case of ancestral histories, the distinction between personal and political becomes elided. Esther's smallpox, caused by political neglect, ultimately becomes the means by which she is able to throw off the past even as her scars bear witness to how, as the novel would have it, all

---

[61] Cynthia Northcutt Malone, '"Flight" and "Pursuit": Fugitive Identity in *Bleak House*', *Dickens Studies Annual*, Spring 1990, Vol. 19, 107–24 (p. 109).

[62] Malone, '"Flight" and "Pursuit"', pp. 112–13.

worlds are related. The point is that the second Bleak House, occupied by Esther and Allan is not the same as the first, meaning that the forces of repetition are in this instance cleansed of Gothic entrapment.

Ideas about the home are central to the positive generation of this new Bleak House and ideas about home and how that might relate to history is one of the topics addressed in *The Old Curiosity Shop* (1841), where Dickens contemplates how the future, rather than the past, provides a different way of thinking about history and genealogy – two issues that were central to the eighteenth-century Gothic of writers such as Walpole and Radcliffe.

Mighall's summary of *Little Dorrit* notes that the novel reveals 'how memory can be a much stronger prison than the ones constructed by the state, and how lives can be blighted by the burden it entails on future generations'.[63] This is also a view that can be applied to the feudal Dedlocks. The present can be compromised because characters are trapped by a past, the burdens of which have the potential to blight later generations. *The Old Curiosity Shop* explores a contrary view by focusing on how a death, of the virtuous Little Nell, might have positive effects on the future. The novel advances another way of undoing the Gothic by casting off the past and engaging with a future which is all the richer because of, rather than despite, Nell's death. The novel argues that death is not necessarily a tragedy, especially when it is not the consequence of overpowering feelings of Gothic entrapment (as they are for Lady Dedlock, for example), 'When Death strikes down the innocent and young, for every fragile form from which he lets the panting spirit free, a hundred virtues rise, in shapes of mercy, charity, and love, to walk the world and bless it'.[64] The dead inspire us and because of this are granted a post-mortem existence. These considerations move us beyond the Gothic to positively contemplate what is inherited from the dead, which is not some form of ancestral burden, but rather a type of morality that challenges the Gothic genealogy which we witnessed in the account of the ancestral portraits of the Dedlocks. In *The Old Curiosity Shop*, this is articulated in a story told by a coach-riding traveler in which he addresses the apparent tragedy of the death of a young wife and mother:

> 'If you have seen the picture-gallery of any one old family, you will remember how the same face and figure – often the fairest and slightest of them all – come upon you in different generations; and how you trace the same sweet girl through a long line of portraits – never growing old or changing – the Good Angel of the race – abiding by them in all reverses – redeeming all their sins – In this daughter the mother lived again'. (p. 525)

---

[63] Mighall, 'Dickens and the Gothic', p. 90.

[64] Charles Dickens, *The Old Curiosity Shop* (Harmondsworth: Penguin, 2000), p. 544. Further reference to this novel will be inserted parenthetically in the text.

This is not the type of Gothic genealogy that we see haunting characters in *Great Expectations*, *Little Dorrit* and *Bleak House*, but that is not to say that *The Old Curiosity Shop* is without a Gothic presence. Quilp is one such Gothic figure and his erotically tinged pursuit of Little Nell clearly casts him as a Gothic villain, but history also plays a role in this. The narratorial voice of the novel indicates that what is found within the Old Curiosity Shop is a type of ancestral clutter, 'There were suits of mail standing like ghosts in armour here and there, fantastic carvings brought from monkish cloisters, rusty weapons of various kinds, distorted figures in china and wood and iron and ivory: tapestry and strange furniture that might have been designed in dreams' (p. 13). This is a place which is 'cold, and lifeless' (p. 19) and represented as a Gothic space in which the narrator wonders if Nell's grandfather might be capable of 'villainy of the worst kind' in an area of London which might be characterised by 'dark and secret deeds' (p. 20). Nell appears as 'So very young, so spiritual, so slight and fairy-like' and the danger to her is prompted by 'the heaps of fantastic things I had seen huddled together' in the shop (p. 20). For the narrator 'she seemed to exist in a kind of allegory' (p. 22) even as he imagines her as 'alone in the midst of all this lumber and decay, and ugly age' (p. 22). Nell is not in quite so much danger as the narrator fears, but it is noteworthy that he ascribes much of the danger to the antiquities found in the shop. For the narrator, Nell is a victim in a Gothic novel held under siege by the forces of the past. She is seemingly physically and psychologically entrapped in this space. This is a space that they lose to Quilp, forcing Nell and her grandfather to become beggars – which provides Dickens with an opportunity to dwell on the present-day horrors of those forced into poverty by the industrial economy. Nell, nevertheless, escapes from the encompassing Gothic history as her death becomes developed into an allegory about death and renewal. The novel thus provides another antidote to the stifling Gothic history that is elaborated through the objects of the past found in the shop. The past and the present are notably Gothic in the novel and Nell is powerless to affect change because, as noted by Theodor Adorno, Nell 'has no power over the world from which she flees'.[65] Reform is not possible in the present but might, optimistically, occur in an imagined future, as the school-master says to Nell 'An infant, a prattling child, dying in its cradle, will live again in the better thoughts of those who loved it; and play a part, through them, in the redeeming actions of the world' (p. 410). History here is a personal matter and begins with the reformation of the individual. These issues are given clear

---

[65] Theodor W. Adorno, 'On Dickens' *The Old Curiosity Shop*: A Lecture', *Notes to Literature*, Vol. 2 (New York: Columbia University Press, 1992), pp. 171–77, p. 177.

political treatment in Dickens' historical novels *Barnaby Rudge* (1841) and *A Tale of Two Cities* (1859).

Barnaby Rudge focuses on the anti-Catholic Gordon Riots of 1780 and makes repeated use of images of phantoms and prison cell psychologies to demonstrate how a damaging set of beliefs permeates people, places and institutions. The novel culminates in a series of riots which suggest the apocalypse. In the final riots, the rioters are described as burning in a lake of flaming alcoholic spirits which they attempt to consume even as it leads to their destruction:

> While some stooped with their lips to the brink and never raised their heads again, others sprang up from the fiery draught, and danced, half in a mad triumph, and half in the agony of suffocation, until they fell, and steeped their corpses in the liquor that had killed them.[66]

The scene represents the horror of the mob and crowds and their role in historical events is a topic that Dickens returned to in his reflections on the French Revolution in *A Tale of Two Cities*. In the later novel, as in *Barnaby Rudge*, individuals participate in rebellious events due to political, but also often deeply personal, reasons. Personal malevolence is never very far from some forms of ostensible radical political motivation such as the actions of the vengeful Madame Defarge who is determined that Charles Darnay should be executed because his aristocratic father and uncle were responsible for abuses of power in the ancien régime, including the imprisonment of Dr Manette who wanted to report them for their crimes. To that degree, the novel articulates the Walpolean Gothic relating to the sins of the fathers being passed on to their sons. The novel also suggests a solution to this which relies on a language of doubling which is initially suggested in the dialectical language that we find in the novel's opening lines:

> It was the best of times, it was the worst of times, it was the age of wisdom, it was the age of foolishness, it was the epoch of belief, it was the epoch of incredulity, it was the season of Light, it was the season of Darkness, it was the spring of hope, it was the winter of despair we had everything before us, we had nothing before us, we were all going direct to Heaven, we were all going direct the other way – in short, the period was so far like the present period, that some of its noisiest authorities insisted on its being received, for good or for evil, in the superlative degree of comparison only.[67]

Albert D. Hutter has noted how this 'establishes the "twoness" of everything to follow: characters are twinned and doubled and paired; the setting is doubled' and 'the historical perspective is divided between an eighteenth-century event

---

[66] Charles Dickens, *Barnaby Rudge* (Harmondsworth: Penguin, 1986), p. 618.

[67] Charles Dickens, *A Tale of Two Cities* (Harmondsworth: Penguin, 1989), p. 35. Further reference to this novel will be inserted parenthetically in the text.

and its nineteenth-century apprehensions'.[68] This echoes the issue about doubling which we witnessed in the previous section in an account of death-cell psychology. Freud's version of the uncanny double is suggested here, and it is the doubling between Darnay and Sydney Carton which has attracted the most critical attention even while the novel also addresses the issue of the psychological effects of incarceration on Dr Manette which implicates a more familiar form of doubling, discussed in the previous section.

It is Dr Manette's plight which the novel initially addresses in Gothic terms as he is described as representing the return of the dead, now released from his entombment after having been 'buried alive for eighteen years!' (p. 48). His estranged daughter, Lucie, is apprehensive about this reunion 'I am going to see his Ghost! It will be his Ghost – not him!' (p. 57). Later, she finds it difficult to conceive of her father in human terms. While in France she says to Defarge, who has helped to liberate her father that 'I am afraid of it'...'Of it? What?' 'I mean of him. Of my father' (p. 69). In their first meeting Dr Manette places his 'spectral face upon her warm young breast' in an act which makes her his symbolic mother who can bring him 'back to life and hope' (p. 74). Later Dr Manette admits to Lucie that he was often haunted by an image of her in his prison cell that both was and was not her. This phantom was like Lucie 'but not the same' (p. 219) as it was a projected spectre of the type that more malevolently appears in *The American Notes*' account of solitary confinement. Dr Manette is haunted by the trauma of his incarceration and at moments of crisis lapses back into shoe-making (his prison employment) as a way of negotiating trauma. This Gothic narrative is paralleled by the alternative ostensible Gothic narrative which centres on doubling.

In the opening paragraph of the novel, it is noted that the turmoil of the French Revolution was 'so far like the present period' that the nature of the historical narrative is thrown into question. The present is read through the prism of the past and vice versa and this has implications for how we read the doubleness that is established between Darnay and Carton, who are doubles as they resemble each other and because they are love rivals (although Lucie is only in love with Darnay). They are not, however, figures who are otherwise clearly linked. The paradox is that 'Dickens explores the ramifications of doubleness from a base that seems confident about individual identity', so that seeing off the double becomes the psychological guarantor of identity.[69] Indeed, once the novel has hinted that Carton might be employed to rescue

---

[68] Albert D. Hutter, 'Nation and Generation in *A Tale of Two Cities*' in Harold Bloom (ed.), *Modern Critical Interpretations: A Tale of Two Cities* (New York: Chelsea House, 1987), pp. 37–56, p. 50.

[69] Susan K. Gillman and Robert L. Patten, 'Dickens: Doubles: Twins: Twains', *Nineteenth-Century Fiction*, March 1985, Vol. 39, No. 4, 441–56 (p. 441).

Darnay 'the text begins to show the reader just how unalike they really are'.[70] This leads to the conclusion that 'part of the doubling in *A Tale of Two Cities* is resolved by annihilating the double'.[71] This produces a different form of doubling than the model produced in the prison cell. For Freud, the double represents the return of the repressed and so implicates the past in the formation of the present. This narrative can be related to Darnay who is a descendant of a corrupt regime, but this only works superficially because he has cast off that regime, is clearly virtuous, and is only arraigned for execution through a vindictive association with the past. He is a figure who has attempted to leave the past behind and is not legitimately implicated in that past. The drama of the historical novel is replaced by a more immediate drama about identity which is maintained, as Ahmed Diaa Dardir notes above, by the casting off of the double, as far as doubling, pace Freud, can be seen as about the return of the repressed. This is a different formation of doubling founded not on similarity but rooted within the lexical formulations of the antitheses which characterise the opening of the novel. Carton, drunk at a dinner party, is conscious of Darnay's negative judgment of him. After Darnay leaves, Carton looks at himself in a mirror and ponders his feelings about Darnay:

> 'Do you particularly like the man?' he muttered, at his own image; 'why should you particularly like a man who resembles you? There is nothing in you to like; you know that. Ah, confound you! What a change you have made in yourself! A good reason for taking to a man, that he shows you what you have fallen away from, and what you might have been! Change places with him, and would you have been looked at by those blue eyes as he was, and commiserated by that agitated face as he was? Come on, and have it out in plain words! You hate the fellow'. (p. 116)

Carton's view that he compares unfavourably with Darnay prompts him to occupy his space on the scaffold. He knows that this is a way in which he can save a good man and acquire the redemption that Carton so clearly craves. His Christ-like sacrifice symbolically ensures his immortality as in the closing passage of the novel he envisages a role in which he lives on through the child that Lucie and Darnay will in the future have, a child 'who bears my name' whom he imagines growing into 'a man winning his way up in that path of life which once was mine. I see him winning it so well, that my name is made illustrious there by the light of his' (p. 404). *A Tale of Two Cities* is thus a novel

---

[70] Matthew Crofts, 'Dickens's Gothic Double: *A Tale of Two Cities* and Watts Phillips's *The Dead Heart*', *Victoriographies*, 2018, Vol. 8, No. 3, 290–306 (p. 304).

[71] Ahmed Diaa Dardir, 'Fascination and Terror: Orientalism and the Return of the Repressed in *A Tale of Two Cities* and "A Christmas Tree"', *Dickens Quarterly*, September 2022, Vol. 39, No. 3, 338–58 (p. 356).

which looks towards the future as a way of renouncing the past. Gothic doubling becomes transformed into an account of redemption and rebirth (as far as Carton sees himself as reflected in Lucie and Darnay's projected baby). The Gothic entrapments of the past are finally laid to rest in an historical novel.

A Tale of Two Cities appears to represent a new type of doubling, seemingly employed to challenge the type of Gothic self-hauntings which populate *Bleak House*. Susan K. Gillman and Robert L. Pattern, itemise the different formations of doubling in Dickens from the 'coincidental doubles in *A Tale of Two Cities*, to feigned doubles in *Our Mutual Friend* … to ontogenetic doubles in *Great Expectations*'.[72] In *A Tale of Two Cities* the 'internalised warfare between the demonic energies of the unconscious and the civilising repressions of the conscious', are transposed on to the French Revolution itself, so making political formations of rebellion Gothic because they pursue corrupt personal agendas which stand in marked contrast to Carton's honourable self-sacrifice.[73] Ultimately, the prison-house of history is capable of being cast off, Dr Manette's regressions into shoe-making notwithstanding, because love functions as an antidote to Gothic entrapment albeit in a novel which is 'one of [Dickens'] most Gothic works'.[74] Typically in Dickens the Gothic is asserted as a type of blockage to social reform, only for him to suggest ways in which these moments of physical and psychological incarceration can be eluded. Trying to find a way to envisage a better future, as Carton does in his final moments, becomes key to establishing the reformation of the self and the society which would otherwise hold back the subject in repetitious patterns of self-destruction. This is why Carton imagines his rebirth in a narrative about 'winning' which takes place in a projected future.

The ghosts of the past generate complex patterns of entrapment and Dickens explores ways in which characters can overcome these regressive Gothic forces. Dickens' ghost stories provide another way of reflecting on images of emotional and psychological imprisonment. The problem posed by the ghost relates closely to the issue of sight. To see clearly is to identify the places of reform, an issue addressed in *Bleak House*, and how this relates to the ghost stories is addressed in the following section.

3 Ghosts

The figure of the ghost has played an important part in the earlier discussions of prisons and history. There we witnessed how subjects are made spectral by

---

[72] Gillman and Patten, 'Dickens: Doubles', p. 447.
[73] Gillman and Patten, 'Dickens: Doubles', p. 448.
[74] Crofts, 'Dickens's Gothic Doubles', p. 292.

forms of incarceration which generate haunted, traumatic, states. In the prison cell, the prisoner is buried alive and this liminal condition is expressed in the spectral form which they have become. History has a similar effect as the repetition of the past indicates that characters are haunted by social obligations and complex family dramas. What is inherited from the past is a spectral burden that characters need to cast off in order to reclaim their lives by looking forward to an untroubled future. The idea of inheriting a pressure from the past is also reflected in Dickens' view of the form of the ghost story.

In 'A Christmas Tree' (1850) Dickens reflected on the nature of story-telling and the ghost story where his narrator seemingly laments the limitations of the form:

> There is no end to the old houses, with resounding galleries, and dismal state bedchambers, and haunted wings shut up for many years, through which we may ramble, with an agreeable creeping up our back, and encounter any number of ghosts, but (it is worthy of remark perhaps) reducible to a very few general types and classes; for, ghosts have little originality, and 'walk' in a beaten track.[75]

Ghosts appear as overly familiar forms devoid of Gothic terror because any fear is 'agreeable' and closer to the idea of the cosy fireside tale than Gothic formations of horror and transgression. Dickens, however, does innovate the form because many of Dickens' ghost stories, while not obviously Gothic, are employed to promote his social reformist agenda and employ the ghost story to channel a clear political message. As we shall see, in the ghost stories (especially in the Christmas books) the spectres are frequently figures associated with developing a reformist mentality (as in Jacob Marley's ghost in *A Christmas Carol* [1843], for example). These are ghosts which help those who are in danger of becoming Gothic figures, like Scrooge, who is socially and morally spectral because he has cut himself off from society by scorning ideas about a shared humanity and charitable reform. The ghosts, in this instance, function to arrest the Gothic and to socially integrate otherwise alienated characters by prompting them to engage with social reform. This is a different type of spectre than that found in the self-haunting that we have witnessed in accounts of death-cell psychology, or in accounts of the dead hand of the past. These are tales of redemption in which the ghost is both a warning and a guide. Not all of Dickens' ghosts behave like this and this section explores examples which contribute to a Gothic language of entrapment that we have seen elsewhere, in which characters have become lost souls who cannot be redeemed. Ghosts are not

---

[75] Charles Dickens, "'Christmas Ghosts' from 'A Christmas Tree'" in *The Signalman & Other Ghost Stories* (Stroud: Alan Sutton, 1990), pp. 110–16, p. 112.

monolithic entities in Dickens; he uses them for different purposes and with different types of political positions in mind and this is illustrated by whether they are used Gothically, or not.

Dickens in 'A Christmas Tree' may strike a pessimistic note about the limits of the ghost story, but ghost stories are a key feature of the nineteenth-century Gothic tradition and their nuancing by Dickens for comedic, narrative, and social reformist affect influenced a later generation of ghost story writers who saw that Dickens had indeed shown how ghosts manifest a challenging 'originality'. The appearance of ghosts in *The Pickwick Papers* (1837), indicates that they can be both serious and comic.

It was noted in the earlier discussion of *The Pickwick Papers* that the interpolated narratives often address issues about confinement and that this, following the work of Steven Marcus, stands in opposition to the freedoms of expression and physical movement which characterises the main body of the novel. There are nine such interpolated tales in the novel and while not all of them qualify as ghost stories many of them do, as in 'The Story of the Bagman's Uncle' which was discussed in the Introduction. The initial focus of this section is on 'The Story of the Goblins Who Stole a Sexton' as it anticipates many of the themes explored in *A Christmas Carol*, a novella which articulates Dickens' social reformist agenda, which is also a feature of his later Christmas books, especially *The Chimes* (1844), and *The Haunted Man* (1848).

Gabriel Grub, the Sexton, is an early version of Scrooge. The tale, set on Christmas Eve, finds Grub responding antagonistically to the prevailing Christmas cheer, especially when the sight of boisterous children leads him to think of 'measles, scarlet fever, thrush, whooping-cough, and a good many other sources of consolation besides' (p. 381). Grub is digging a grave when he comes across a goblin sitting on a tombstone who, with other goblins, are intent on punishing Grub for his meanness towards children. These goblins are other-worldly entities that, in their association with redemptive visions, function like Dickens' typical Christmas spectres. In a series of scenes which foreshadow Scrooge's visit to the Cratchits, Grub is shown a vision of a poor family with a dying child. When the boy dies the family is not destroyed by their grief because 'they knew that he was an angel looking down upon, and blessing them, from a bright and happy Heaven' (p. 387). Grub is shown a later vision in which the parents cheerfully relate 'old stories of earlier and bygone days' (p. 387) to their family before the parents die and are mourned by their descendants who gain solace in the idea 'that they should one day meet again' (p. 387). This is a sentiment which as we saw in Section 2, also colours the reflections on the death of Little Nell. Grub's visions demonstrate the indefatigability of the human spirit in which people overcome their feelings of privation 'because they bore within their own bosoms the materials of happiness, contentment and peace' (pp. 388–89), which is in stark contrast to 'men like himself, who snarled at the mirth and cheerfulness of others' and consequently 'were the foulest weeds on the fair surface of the earth . . . setting all the good of the world against the evil' (p. 389). In keeping with many of the other Gothic tales in *The Pickwick Papers*, Grub's visions seem to have come to him in a drink-addled dream, but on awakening 'he was an altered man, and he could not bear the thought of returning to a place where his repentance would be scoffed at, and his reformation disbelieved' (p. 389), and he leaves the town. Grub, unlike Scrooge, is seemingly beyond reaccommodation within the community, who quickly attribute his disappearance to the goblins and his departure becomes romantically mythologised by 'some very credible witnesses who had distinctly seen him whisked through the air on the back of a chestnut horse blind in one eye, with the hind-quarters of a lion, and the tail of a bear' (p. 389). For all that there is a moral at work here when Grub concludes 'it was a very decent and respectable sort of world after all' (p. 389), which had been tarnished by his self-generated misery.

The community's attempt to mythologise his absence is undermined 'by the unlooked-for reappearance of Gabriel Grub himself, some ten years afterwards, a ragged contented, rheumatic old man' (p. 390). The community is keen to attribute Grub's vision to a drunken dream and to maintain the romantic view of his abduction, which undermines his moral enlightenment. The conclusion suggests that Grub may have gained an epiphany in his drink-addled misery which made him a better person but he cannot expect others to believe him. In this tale, the spectral goblins take on a non-Gothic form as they provide Grub with a view of the world which stimulates feelings of empathy which stop Grub turning into the Gothic monster of the text. Grub is in danger of becoming soulless, which also implicates a Christian vision as the key to salvation. Grub needs to see the world differently in order to be redeemed and in this process the putatively Gothic Goblins become recuperated.

The importance of vision and how to see social solutions is also central to *A Christmas Carol* which inherits many of the issues addressed in 'The Story of the Goblins Who Stole a Sexton'.[76] How to re-envision the world is central to *A Christmas Carol*, which requires Scrooge to generate a new reality that quashes his utilitarian assessment of how the poor should be treated. At the start of the novella Scrooge exists within a fog-bound world, 'The fog came pouring in at every chink and keyhole, and was so dense without, that although

---

[76] See my *The Ghost Story 1840–1920: A Cultural History* (Manchester: Manchester University Press, 2010), pp. 32–48 where I also discuss a number of the texts explored here.

the court was of the narrowest, the houses opposite were mere phantoms'.[77]
These fogs are closely linked to the spirits of the departed, like Marley's spectral
face which 'had a dismal light about it, like a bad lobster in a dark cellar' (p. 54).
The ghosts are lost souls who are bound by their past material lives 'The air was
filled with phantoms' and 'Every one of them wore chains . . . none were free',
their 'misery with them all was, clearly, that they sought to interfere, for good, in
human matters, and had lost the power for ever' (p. 65). Wealth in this spectral
form is useless as it cannot transform the lives of others. For Scrooge 'Whether
these creatures faded into mist, or mist enshrouded them, he could not tell'
(p. 65), as they become part of the fog. Tellingly these lost spirits are different to
the three spirits that Scrooge encounters, which bring with them an enlightenment that prompts Scrooge to see the world more clearly, reflected in Scrooge's
view from his window on awakening on Christmas morning, 'No fog, no mist;
clear, bright, jovial, stirring, cold; cold, piping for the blood to dance to; Golden
sunlight; Heavenly sky; sweet fresh air; merry bells' (p. 128). The implication is
that these fogs are mental fogs and that what is required is a change of
perception, an idea that Dickens employs, as discussed in Section 1, to reflect
on Chancery in *Bleak House*.

The temporal spirits in *A Christmas Carol* have a purpose to them and even
the human ghosts generate sympathy because they are tragic figures who find
out all too late that they are unable to make a charitable intervention into the
world. The novella centres on the importance of the redistribution of money and
this is an issue which has divided critical opinion. A Marxian view would see
Scrooge's reintegration into society and his willingness to spend as a shoring up
of the market economy rather than an argument for the necessity of a radical re-
evaluation of it that the child-like figures of Ignorance and Want imply. Ruth
Glancy, however, while acknowledging Thomas Carlyle's dismissal of
A Christmas Carol (because it suggested that happiness could be secured by
access to a Turkey dinner), argues that 'its attack on the breakdown of the
humane relationship between masters and men with the rise of the Industrial
Revolution' shared something with Carlyle's *Past and Present* (1843), although
minus the medievalism.[78] There is a paradox here, at an abstract level Scrooge's
redemption is illustrated by his preparedness to spend (to put money into
circulation), while his improved relations with Bob Cratchit seem to centre on

---

[77] Charles Dickens, *A Christmas Carol* in Michael Slater (ed.), *The Christmas Books*, Vol. 1
(Harmondsworth: Penguin, 1985), pp. 45–134, p. 47. Further reference to this novella will be
inserted parenthetically in the text.

[78] Ruth Glancy, 'Christmas Books and Stories' in John Jordan, Robert L. Patten and
Catherine Waaters (eds.), *The Oxford Handbook of Charles Dickens* (Oxford: Oxford
University Press, 2018), pp. 191–206, p. 194.

workers' rights. The social reformist agenda of *A Christmas Carol* indicates that the ghost story can be used to challenge political and economic realities. However, the use of the Gothic is not as straightforward as this implies. The presence of horror is associated with Scrooge's early determination to remain a miser entombed with his money and so rendering himself, the tale suggests, a spectral living dead figure whose isolation from the world has rendered him subhuman. This Scrooge is clearly the Gothic monster of the text and it indicates that being a monster makes you see the world in a certain, foggy, way. It is important that a socially transformative redemption becomes possible, a theme which Dickens returned to in *The Chimes*.

In *The Chimes* the otherwise big-hearted figure of Toby Veck is moved to despondency after reading negative newspaper accounts of the plights of the poor, leading him to conclude 'I get so puzzled sometimes that I am not even able to make up my mind whether there is any good at all in us, or whether we are born bad'.[79] Later, after reading about a poor woman who killed her child before committing suicide he exclaims 'Unnatural and cruel! None but people who were bad at heart: born bad: who had no business on the earth: could do such deeds' (p. 196). Veck is seemingly summoned by bells to his local church. They appear to call him by name as though they had a message for him, this is a nightmare vision in which 'He saw the tower, whither his charmed footsteps had brought him, swarming with dwarf phantoms, spirits, elfin creatures of the Bells' (p. 201). These spirits of the bells represent the diversity of human experience in which 'He saw them, ugly, handsome, crippled, exquisitely formed. He saw them young, he saw them old, he saw them kind, he saw them cruel' (p. 201). This fanciful vision is again imbued with reality, but the dream becomes a nightmare in which Toby seemingly dies after falling from the tower. His spirit is then shown a number of scenes focusing on his daughter Meg, her husband Richard, and an acquaintance called Will and his daughter, Lilian. Toby watches their progress over a number of years and sees Lilian drift into prostitution, Richard dying an alcoholic, and Meg's contemplation of infanticide and suicide (glossing what Toby had earlier read in the newspaper). The bells prompt Toby in a way similar to the Christmas spirits in *A Christmas Carol*, they urge him to 'keep a good heart' (p. 162), against the negative representations of the poor, leading a bell to articulate the moral of the story, that one 'Who turns his back upon the fallen and disfigured of his kind; abandons them as Vile; and does not trace and track with pitying eyes the unfenced precipice by which they fell from Good' (p. 206). On seeing Meg

---

[79] Charles Dickens, *The Chimes* in Michael Slater (ed.), *The Christmas Books*, Vol. 1 (Harmondsworth: Penguin, 1985), pp. 148–245, p. 158. Further reference to this novella will be inserted parenthetically in the text.

contemplate suicide Toby pleads for mercy 'in this hour, if, in my love for her, so young and good, I slandered Nature in the breasts of mothers rendered desperate!' (p. 240). In keeping with Dickens' other stories about spirits the end reveals that this has all been a dream of Toby's with the added twist that his restoration to happiness may also be considered a possible dream, although one which is grounded in truth with the reader asked 'to bear in mind the stern realities from which these shadows come' (p. 245), a conclusion which suggests that again there is a possible divine provenance at work with Toby who was summoned to the Church. The tale provides another example of how spirits articulate a message of redemption by instilling a socially transformative vision. What is truly Gothic is the way in which Veck blames social and economic victims for their plights. As we have seen in Dickens, mindsets and mentalities are just as Gothic as institutions and histories. Spectres here are non-Gothic spirits who provide enlightenment and understanding. The supernatural is thus used to support a Christian cosmology of transformation and redemption in which reactionary critique is exposed as a form of political negligence (an issue which, as we have seen, Dickens explored in depth in *Bleak House*).

Dickens' Christmas spirits possess a clear, if broadly formulated, reformist zeal which enables characters like Scrooge and Toby Veck to reconnect with their families and the wider social world in which family life takes place. Dickens' Christmas book of 1848 *The Haunted Man* addresses ideas about doubling and selfhood which contribute to a Gothic exploration of whether horror is generated from within, or outside of the self, one which R.L. Stevenson tacitly inherits in the *Strange Case of Dr Jekyll and Mr Hyde* (1886). Dickens' haunted man, Redlaw, like Stevenson's Dr Jekyll, is trained in Chemistry. Redlaw reflects on the hardships he has endured to progress in his profession. He feels bitter about his past and blames its privations for his feelings of despair, which generates a version of himself that appears in his room (evocative of the scene of self-haunting in the *American Notes*). He notes 'its appalling copy of his face looking where his face looked, and bearing the expression his face bore'.[80] The emphasis on 'looking' in the scene glosses, and reverses, the significance of sight in the earlier Christmas books in which visions enable Scrooge and Toby Veck to see the world differently. Here the challenge posed by sight is confrontational and constitutes an uneasy moment of self-reflection in which Redlaw 'turned suddenly, and stared upon the Ghost. The Ghost, as sudden in its motion … stared on him' (p. 264). This ghost demands that Redlaw 'Look upon me!' (p. 266) as he sums up Redlaw's life as one of self-

---

[80] Charles Dickens, *The Haunted Man* in Michael Slater (ed.), *The Christmas Books*, Vol. 2 (Harmondsworth: Penguin, 1985), pp. 244–353, p. 264. Further reference to this novella will be inserted parenthetically in the text.

denial that also crucially centres on his neglect of a sister who had loved him and the feelings of loss and guilt that this generates. The ghost provokes Redlaw to exclaim 'Let me forget it … Let me blot if from my memory' (p. 267). The ghost, on request, cancels all of Redlaw's unhappy memories but this gift becomes a curse, because without these memories he is without a conscience and additionally will 'henceforth destroy its like in all whom you approach' (p. 271). Initially, Redlaw is confused by his inability to empathise, noting that 'My mind is going blind!' (p. 294), and he becomes unable to relate to personal items in his rooms which recollect his past 'Now, they were but objects' (p. 295). He becomes dehumanised and pleads with the phantom 'Give me back *my*self!' (p. 305, italics in original). The restoration of his memory brings him back to life and those around him whose memories he had erased. Here memory becomes positive, whereas, as we have seen, in *Little Dorrit* and *A Tale of Two Cities*, memory is negative because it evokes a Gothic past. Again, a ghost is used in order to banish the Gothic by sanitising memory and using it for redemptive purposes because by suppressing feeling Redlaw becomes inhuman and his redemption is similar to that of Scrooge. However, it is the inward turn that is revealing. Ghosts can be found within in this tale and what is found within is a trauma that can only be corrected by developing an empathetic social awareness. The inner life is a troubled one in Dickens, as we saw with Bill Sikes wrestling with his conscience after the murder of Nancy, it may come too late. It was an idea that Dickens explored further in 'The Hanged Man's Bride, or A Ghost in the Bride's Chamber' from *The Lazy Tour of Two Idle Apprentices*, co-authored with Wilkie Collins in 1857.

The Lazy Tour of Two Idle Apprentices includes two interpolated ghost stories, one told to Goodchild by a Dr Speddie about one Arthur Halliday and the other, which is discussed here, the often anthologised 'The Hanged Man's Bride', about the ghost of a murderer who talks to Goodchild. 'The Hanged Man's Bride' is notably devoid of a concluding moral redemption. The topic of sight and money, which runs throughout the ghost stories discussed here is again apparent. Idle and Goodchild stay at a hotel that has been converted from an older house, where they discover an eccentric occupant. The initial encounter with this figure is related by Goodchild who asks the, at this point seemingly human, resident, 'I had the pleasure, I believe, of seeing you, yesterday?', meeting a non-committal response Goodchild perseveres 'I think you saw me. Did you not', which is met with 'Saw *you*? … O yes, I saw *you*. But, I see many who never see me'.[81] The man's eyes are the focus of attention, he seems

---

[81] Charles Dickens and Wilkie Collins, *The Lazy Tour of Two Idle Apprentices* (New York: J.W. Lovell, 1884), p. 247, italics in original. Further reference to this text will be inserted parenthetically in the text.

'unable to wink, as if his eyelids had been nailed to his forehead' with the eyes described as 'two spots of fire' (p. 247). How to see and how one looks were used for reformist ends in the Christmas books, but here the moral and political status of looking is developed for Gothic affect rather than in support of a serious moral agenda. The old man begins his tale and uses his eyes to add expression to it, which suggests a quasi-mesmeric influence with Goodchild believing 'that he saw threads of fire stretch from the old man's eyes to his own, and there attach themselves' (p. 249). The man's tale centres on how he defrauded the daughter of a woman that he had pursued by forging the woman's will so that she leaves her money to her ten-year-old daughter, Ellen. Ellen is raised with the expectation that the man will become her husband. When that happens she is forced to write out a document leaving her money to him. He then commands her to die. Ellen is described by the man as 'A weak, credulous, incapable, helpless nothing' (p. 249), who can be easily persuaded to die. The power of the man's gaze is emphasised, he does not have to say die and notes the effects of 'looking the word at her' (p. 254). When she dies he is confronted by a young man who had been in love with Ellen and who had witnessed the man's poor treatment of her. In order to silence him the man murders him and buries him at the base of a tree which, sometime after, is struck by lightning and when the body is exposed the man is tried and executed.

The man's ghost appears throughout the month in which he was executed and on every hour the ghost replicates itself until there are twelve versions of him. This escalation echoes the financial success that the man had achieved after the death of Ellen:

> ... he turned his money over and over, and still over. He was in the dark trade, and gold-dust trade ... In ten years, he had turned his money over, so many times, that the traders and shippers who had dealings with him ... declared that he had increased his fortune, twelve hundred per cent. (p. 259)

The ghosts are generated out of this 'dark trade' as he becomes punished not for the murder but for the disinheritance. This ghost (or ghosts) is devoid of humour, they are amoral and avaricious and represent the presence of an illegitimate economy. The ghost can only be laid to rest if they tell their tale to two strangers, but as Idle fell asleep and did not hear the story, the curse is not lifted. In order to escape it requires Goodchild to shake off what are now the penetrating gazes of two ghosts, 'he struggled so hard to get free from the four fiery threads, that he snapped them' (p. 265). He thus manages to escape these eyes before they can entrap him into this Gothic world. Looking and being looked at is a recurring theme in the ghost stories and Dickens returned to it in a later Christmas story, 'The Signalman' which appeared as part of the portmanteau narrative *Mugby*

Junction published in the extra Christmas number of *All the Year Round* in 1866. 'The Signalman' examines forms of entrapment in a self-reflective way which provides a meta-analysis of the whole issue of entrapment which has been explored throughout this book.

The narrator of the tale encounters the signalman in a deep railway cutting shortly after a train has passed through it. In speaking to the man it is clear that he is beset by doubts about how to read the signs of danger which his job compels him to monitor. He initially associates the narrator with a presage of danger by linking him to the red light near the mouth of the tunnel. He tells the narrator, who had commented on the look of dread on the signalman's face, that 'I was doubtful ... whether I had seen you before'.[82] This is related to the signalman's concern that he had on three occasions seen a spectral figure that seems to warn him about an impending railway crash. The signalman, however, is unsure if this spectral figure is real or not and this points towards the crux of the story when he tells the narrator 'what troubles me so dreadfully is the question, What does the spectre mean?' (p. 10). This is a question which runs throughout all of the texts discussed in this section and it is clearly central to Dickens' idea about subjectivity, interpretation, and social reform. *Bleak House* emphasises the importance of seeing through the fog of chancery in order to make the necessary links which identify political neglect as the cause of the pestilence which emanates from Tom-all-Alone's. The clarity of the detective vision of Inspector Bucket parallels this as it too provides a way of seeing which sees through, and so resolves, other forms of mystery. This is a position which the signalman is unable to occupy precisely because he cannot interpret the signs (the signals) that are seemingly spectrally sent to him. The problem is that his work requires 'exactness and watchfulness' (p. 3), attributes that he singularly lacks and which can be attributed to his socially liminal position.

The narrator notes of the signalman that, 'He had been, when young (if I could believe it, sitting in that hut,—he scarcely could), a student of natural philosophy, and had attended lectures; but he had run wild, misused his opportunities, gone down, and never risen again' (p. 4). His job requires very little labour and he spends much of his time in half-hearted intellectual pursuits:

> He had taught himself a language down here, – if only to know it by sight, and to have formed his own crude ideas of its pronunciation, could be called learning it. He had also worked at fractions and decimals, and tried a little algebra; but he was, and had been as a boy, a poor hand at figures. (p. 3)

---

[82] Charles Dickens, 'The Signalman' in *The Signalman & Other Ghost Stories* (Stroud: Alan Sutton, 1990), pp. 1–13, p. 3. Further reference to this tale will be inserted parenthetically in the text.

This very partial understanding of things makes him prone to misreading the signs of danger that he is professionally obligated to monitor. His is a form of entrapment which comes out of this inability to master the world in which he finds himself. The problem is that he is physically isolated at the bottom of the deep cutting in which his hut is located. He is unable to see beyond the railway line and its tunnel which suggests a form of entrapment which is compounded by his inability to mentally escape (reflected in his imperfectly mastered knowledges) from this predicament. Repetition also plays a role in this.

The signalman's initial wariness about the narrator was because the narrator's opening greeting of 'Halloa! Below there!' (p. 1) is a repetition of the phrase used previously by a figure that the signalman had seen one night beside the tunnel entrance. He recalls that this figure, 'stood just outside the blackness of the tunnel. I advanced so close upon it that I wondered at its keeping the sleeve across its eyes. I ran right up at it, and had my hand stretched out to pull the sleeve away, when it was gone' (p. 7). This is a figure associated with a type of blindness (that 'sleeve across its eyes'), which reflects on the signalman's inability to see the signs of danger. The narrator attributes this vision of blindness to a medical problem, 'I showed him how that this figure must be a deception of his sense of sight; and how that figures, originating in disease of the delicate nerves that minister to the functions of the eye, were known to have often troubled patients' (p. 7). The problem of how to see and interpret is closely related to that pressing problem of 'What does the spectre mean?' (p. 10) which, in the ghost stories and in a novel such as *Bleak House*, identifies spectrality as key to understanding the symbolic truths (about identity, history, and politics) articulated within those texts. Esther Summerson may have a moment of epiphany on the ghost's walk at Chesney Wold, but the signalman is trapped within a narrative in which he merely sees forms of blindness which reflect on his inability to properly read the signs of danger, which makes his death seem inevitable when he is run down by a train. In the accident, the train driver shouts out 'Below there! Look out!' and states that at last he put his 'arm before my eyes not to see' (p. 13) the final collision. So, in the end the very vision that the signalman had seen earlier becomes real but, typically, he has misread the danger.

'The Signalman' is about the failure of sight and interpretation. It represents another form of Gothic entrapment in which a subject becomes adrift in the world because they have lost all confidence in their ability to understand that world. Srdjan Smajic's exploration of the role of sight in the ghost story concludes that the 'ghost-seer is typically caught in a disconcerting double bind between instinctive faith in the evidence of one's sight and the troubling knowledge that vision is often deceptive and unreliable'.[83] In Dickens, how-ever, how to see enables you to see the system in a new light. 'The Signalman' can be read as a reflection on the ghost story. It is a meta-critical analysis of the form which identifies seeing clearly as the way out of a world associated with partially mastered forms of knowledge, troubling visions, and cryptic messages.

The signalman is to a degree dehumanised because he is reduced to the function of his role (he is nameless, merely defined by his occupation) which makes him robot-like. John D. Stahl has related the signalman to Frederick S. Williams' *Our Iron Roads* (1852), which outlines the responsibilities of signalmen. Williams argued that 'In the modern interlocking of signals the principle aimed at is, so far as possible, to supersede the man by the machine'.[84] Signs and signals can no longer be made sense of in this new form of industrialisation which begins to take on a life of its own, one which is hostile to the subject. This was an issue also touched upon by Dickens in *Dombey and Son* (1848) when the devious James Carker is killed by a train in an act of retribution. By the time of 'The Signalman' this has turned into a more abstract concern with the modern world and its potential to dehumanise, and so to create spectres – an issue that Dickens had explicitly addressed in 'A December Vision' (1850).

'A December Vision' was published as the lead article in *Household Words* on 14th December 1850. Michael Slater notes that the article should be read 'as a continuation of a recurrent theme in Dickens's Christmas Books' which is 'the failure of the great institutions of Victorian society to address the terrible problems of mass poverty and deprivation'.[85] If ghosts, however, can be appeased or even function as moral guides, as in *A Christmas Carol*, the same cannot be said for the spectre which haunts 'A December Vision', which is the dehumanised and dehumanizing spirit of the industrial economy. The article begins, 'I saw a mighty Spirit, traversing the world without any rest or pause. It was omnipresent, it was all-powerful, it had no compunction, no pity, no relenting sense that any appeal from any of the race of men could reach'.[86] This is a figure which spread pestilence in a way that is reminiscent of the spread

---

[83] Srdjan Smajic, 'The Trouble with Ghost-Seeing: Vision, Ideology, and Genre in the Victorian Ghost Story', *English Literary History*, 2003, Vol. 70, No. 4, 1107–35 (p. 1109).

[84] Frederick S. Williams, *Our Iron Roads: Their History, Construction and Administration* (London: Frank Cass, 1968), pp. 181–82. Cited in John D. Stahl, 'The Source and Significance of the Revenant in Dickens's "The Signal-Man"', *Dickens Studies Newsletter*, 11 (1980), 98–101, 99.

[85] Michael Slater editorial comment on 'A December Vision' in Michael Slater (ed.), *Dickens' Journalism: The Amusements of the People and Other Papers: Reports, Essays and Reviews 1834–1851* (London: Dent, 1996), pp. 305–6, p. 305.

[86] Charles Dickens, 'A December Vision' in Michael Slater (ed.), *Dickens' Journalism: The Amusements of the People and Other Papers: Reports, Essays and Reviews 1834–1851* (London: Dent, 1996), pp. 306–9, p. 306. Further reference to this text will be inserted parenthetically in the text.

of smallpox in *Bleak House*. Tellingly the issue of sight which was closely
aligned with Dickens' social reformist agenda in the other tales about ghosts is
here transformed into looks that can kill all, irrespective of social status as it is
noted 'the Spirit never paused in its appointed work, and, sooner or later, turned
its impartial face on all' (p. 307), because the pollution created by the industrial
economy touches all:

> I saw the rich struck down in their strength, their darling children weakened
> and withered, their marriageable sons and daughters perish in their prime.
> I saw that not one miserable wretch breathed out his poisoned life in the
> deepest cellar of the most neglected town, but, from the surrounding atmos-
> phere, some particles of his infection were borne away, charged with heavy
> retribution on the general guilt. (p. 308)

Death creeps up on everyone unseen until it is too late. The spirit of the
industrial economy is only recognised at the point of death when its gaze is
turned upon you. The question that Dickens raises relates to how it could
become possible to 'see' what the system does, which requires the generation
of a form of radical scepticism that the narrative suggests is both necessary but
seemingly impossible to generate. The invisibility of the system overtakes all,
unless this scepticism can be generated. The problem is the existence of
a widespread acceptance that the inequities of the system need to be tolerated.
Those that can see the system, and here Dickens identifies ministers of state,
ecclesiastics, teachers, and would be social reformers, all pessimistically agree
that 'It is a great wrong – BUT IT WILL LAST MY TIME!' (p. 308), and so do
nothing about it. It is their refusal to change the system which makes them
complicit with the death that is generated by the system. This is a point which
the murderous spirit makes to them when it states that 'Whosoever is
a consenting party to a wrong, comforting himself with the base reflection
that it will last his time, shall bear his portion of that wrong throughout ALL
TIME' (p. 309). In 'A December Vision' Dickens uses the invisibility of
infection as a conceit for the spread of political complacency. The spectre is
machine-like and represents a version of the economic system which stifles any
attempt to generate an alternative vision to it.

The irony is that at the end it is the spectre who makes the point about political
complicity in order to break the cycle of self-destruction. That seeing is crucial
to this change is registered by the narrative voice which can indeed see all of this
which is reflected in the repeated use of 'I saw', which is employed twelve
times. It is the narrator's view that we are asked to engage with it as it holds
political complacency responsible for the unchecked destruction generated by
the industrial economy.

Dickens consistently returns to issues about social reform through the medium of the ghost story. As we have seen, it is in the Christmas books that we witness an emphasis on reform which is only possible if the system is seen in a new way. These transformations are possible and characters and communities can be redeemed. Ghosts function as figures which both draw attention to the need for reform and need to be seen through and exorcised as a way of exorcising the system itself. The spirit of death in 'A December Vision' articulates this position to the complacent when he commands them 'See, each of you' (p. 309), so that they can eradicate him. The death of a way of looking produces the radical scepticism that is required to see the system in a new way and so change it.

This account of ghosts in Dickens has demonstrated that not all such figures should be seen as Gothic forms. It is notable that in the Christmas books the ghost functions as a figure of redemption for Grub, Scrooge, Veck, and Redlaw. These are ostensible Gothic figures that are transformed into benign spirits who enable the principal protagonists to gain redemption and so avoid turning into morally dead-undead Gothic subjects. Learning how to reconnect with society is at the heart of these stories which often include, most explicitly with Scrooge, a reformist agenda. Other ghosts do behave Gothically, in order to demonise those beyond redemption, as in 'The Hanged Man's Bride', or to challenge those who refuse to ameliorate the plight of the victims of the industrial economy, as in 'A December Vision'. How to see the ghost and the visions which it inspires becomes a central device through which Dickens drives issues about social reform. The ghost draws attention to this because its very spectrality both confounds sight (ghosts as visually liminal) and arrests it. Spectres hover around issues of social reform to encourage new ways of looking at the social problems of the period by implicitly asking the question raised in 'The Signalman' 'What does the spectre mean?'.

Conclusion

This Element has addressed the specific way in which Dickens employs the Gothic to identify the social and political forces which stifle social reform. Forms of Gothic entrapment appear in images of physical and mental imprisonment which emphasise the need to reach beyond these constraints as a precondition for embracing radical social change. These issues are addressed at both a social and personal level and by way of conclusion a brief reading of *Great Expectations* (1861) will help to illustrate many of the themes addressed in this Element.

In *Great Expectations*, Pip periodically regards himself as a type of emotional prisoner because he is held back by the traumas of his early years. A visit to

Newgate with Wemmick prompts him to reflect on this legacy, leading him to conclude that 'how strange it was that I should be encompassed by all this taint of prison and crime' (p. 284). Pip, eager to cast this off prior to a meeting with Estella, is struck by the 'contrast between the jail and her' (p. 284), as her beauty and refinement stand in opposition to the corruption and sordidness of the prison. In order to prepare for his meeting Pip 'beat the prison dust off my feet ... and I shook it out of my dress, and I exhaled its air from my lungs' (p. 284). Pip, typically, wants to ensure that he appears as a pristine gentleman and thus an ideal suitor for Estella. The novel, however, suggests that Estella represents another type of entrapment that the unwary Pip needs to negotiate.

Pip's youthful introduction to Satis house provides a prelude to his later encounter with Newgate. The house, 'was of old brick, and dismal, and had a great many iron bars to it. Some of the windows had been walled up; of those that remained, all the lower were rustily barred. There was a court-yard in front, and that was barred' (pp. 84–85). At this point, Estella appears as a type of turnkey who permits Pip entry into the house. The encounter with Miss Havisham represents an encounter with the genius loci of the house, one who corrupts those who come into close contact with her. Her faded white bridal gown and association with death and decay evoke, as James R. Simmons Jr has noted, the scene in Radcliffe's *The Mysteries of Udolpho* (1794) when Emily St. Aubert enters a room at the Château-le-Blanc, in which the Marchioness had died. The room is a time capsule which includes the Marchoness's black veil and various other accoutrements which find their counterpart in Miss Havisham's room, albeit rendered in white, if yellowing, garments.[87] Emily, like Pip, 'describes the tomb-like room in which time has stood still for twenty years'.[88] The black veil was also a crucial feature in Dickens' early foray into the Gothic, 'The Black Veil' (1836), discussed in the Introduction. Simmons notes that while Dickens is clearly indebted to Radcliffe at this moment, there is a fundamental transformation which is signalled in this move from black to white clothing, because 'While Radcliffe's description can be read as little more than exactly what it appears to be, a description of a room tainted by death, Dickens's description of Miss Havisham's chambers becomes much more than that, a look at expectations lost, and expectations thwarted'.[89] To be haunted by Miss Havisham is to be entrapped: an issue made clear in Pip's subsequent dream of her in which, 'A thousand Miss Havishams haunted me. She was on this side of my pillow, on that, at the head of the bed, at the foot, behind the half-opened door of the dressing-

---

[87] This is a different veil to the one Emily had found covering the waxwork.

[88] James R. Simmons Jr, '"Every Discernable Thing in It Was Covered with Dust and Mould": Radcliffe's Château-le-Blanc and Dickens's Satis House', *Dickensian*, Spring 1997, 11–12 (p. 11).

[89] Simmons, 'Dickens's Satis House', p. 12.

room, in the dressing-room, in the room overhead, in the room beneath – everywhere' (p. 325). For Peter Brooks the type of entrapment associated with Miss Havisham is not just about circumscribing Pip's life, it also reflects her ambition to stop time. Her plight represents 'a deviated eroticism which has literally shut out the light, stopped the clocks and made the forward movement of plot impossible'.[90] Escaping the influence of Miss Havisham thus enables Pip to advance into a future beyond her control. The 'deviated eroticism' is, however, projected onto Estella so that the past is never quite cast off because Pip remains enthralled by her. Miss Havisham becomes aware of this when she reflects on what it is that she has passed onto Estella and, by extension, Pip. Her subsequent pleas for forgiveness come too late to save Estella whose heartlessness is generated out of the trauma of Miss Havisham's wedding day abandonment. Miss Havisham is ultimately unable to escape the self-generated prison of Satis House and Pip, in the scene where he wrestles to put out the fire which has engulfed her, becomes complicit in her detention. In an attempt to put out the fire, he wraps her in the sheet which had covered the table for her wedding feast. They find themselves 'on the ground struggling like desperate enemies' (p. 414), in a clear echo of the fight between Magwich and Compeyson. Pip also notes that even when the servants come to help 'I still held her forcibly down with all my strength, like a prisoner who might escape; and I doubt if I even knew who she was, or why we had struggled' (p. 414). It is questionable if, at this stage, Pip's actions suggest that he has forgiven her for misleading him about the identity of his benefactor and for her corruption of Estella. The moment suggests the detention of a criminal trying to flee the scene of a crime. The symbolic point is that Miss Havisham cannot escape Satis House and the history which it contains and Pip will not let her. Brooks notes that her wider attempt to stop time represents the actions 'of the traumatic neurotic whose affects remain fixed on the past, on the traumatic moment which never can be mastered'.[91] The question is whether this inability to master the traumatic moment is inherited by Pip and Estella.

The final section suggests that Pip and Estella may indeed be free of the prison house of Satis house as at the end of the novel it has been demolished and their reunion is staged within the site it once occupied, now cleared for sale as a series of vacant plots. Dickens, famously, struggled with the published ending because the suggestion that Estella and Pip might be romantically brought together at this point contradicts the repeated focus on all the powerful forces which have kept them apart. The closing line of the novel 'I saw no shadow of another parting from her' (p. 493), suggests that, perhaps, Pip did not foresee in

---

[90] Peter Brooks, 'Repetition, and Return: *Great Expectations* and the Study of Plot', *New Literary History*, Spring 1980, Vol. 11, No. 3, 505–26 (p. 508).

[91] Brooks, 'Repetition, and Return', p. 511.

this moment that they might not stay together. Dickens fudges the line but the ambivalence is revealing and takes us back to the section in which Pip visits Newgate. At the end of that section Pip nervously awaits the arrival of Estella, feeling 'contaminated' by the prison setting even as he sees 'her face at the coach window and her hand waving to me' (p. 284). The final concluding one-sentence paragraph records an unformed doubt 'What *was* the nameless shadow which again in that one instant had passed?' (p. 284, italics in original). Does Estella dispel or trail a shadow? At the end of the novel Estella's inability to cast off a shadow can be read as the inability to evade the clutch of the past and this earlier shadow is a herald of that. In the end, Pip is not able to forge the type of connections necessary to relinquish the past. Pip has no real agency as he is lost within the plots of Miss Havisham and Magwich. His voice is ultimately a baffled, alienated, one which has led Annette R. Federico to conclude that the true subject matter of the novel is 'a recognition of human aloneness'.[92] Connections at both a personal and social level have crumbled leaving Pip a victim of a Gothic world which might be physically demolished but which retains a presence through a psychological and emotional introjection which leaves him alone but desperate for some form of belonging.

Great Expectations represents an exercise in the new type of Gothic that Dickens wished to develop. As we have seen, throughout his writing there is a sense that the Gothic provides a form of containment which becomes both psychologically and politically corrosive. The subject is a social being with a private self, but these two worlds need to be bridged if any radical reform is to be instituted. Dickens' focus on forms of physical incarceration always reflects on the psychological and emotional damage that these inflicted. These prison cell scenes have an obvious political charge as they connect the incarcerated subject to the wider forms of injustice that Dickens wants to address as a key political issue that needs to be reformed. Dickens does not, however, simply develop a version of the Gothic in order to explore prison cell psychology. He also develops a form of the Gothic which explores how the past can also function as a form of entrapment. Family histories, as in *Bleak House*, constitute forms of ancestral entrapment that subjects need to move beyond in order to embrace the possibilities of personal and social freedom. This is also a theme of *The Old Curiosity Shop* where the ancestral clutter of the past needs to be left behind in order for a new version of the future to appear – one reflected in the, paradoxically, benevolent affects of Little Nell's death which helps those who wish to lead a better life. How to generate a reformist mentality which can only be manifested against the pull of the past shapes Dickens' employment of the

---

[92] Annette R. Federico, 'Satis House', *Literary Imagination*, Vol. 21, No. 1, 63–76 (p. 75).

Gothic in these examples of history. As we have also seen, it is in the ghost story that we see these issues about the past given sustained treatment. Dickens nuances the ghost story in order to focus on how the spectral presence of the past needs to be combated before subjects, such as Scrooge, become ghosts and so thwarted in their guilty attempts at trying to make amends. In Dickens the ghost enables the subject, and by implication the Victorian reader, to see the economic system in a new way. The ghost draws attention to what is there but not there, the divisive nature of an economic and political system which is sustained by its apparent invisibility. Seeing the world anew requires the development of a social conscience (as in Scrooge's redemption), which enables the possibility of social reform, even while in the case of *A Christmas Carol* it does not encourage the wholesale overthrow of an economic system, but merely encourages a more benign form of redistributive capitalism.

Dickens' Gothic represents a new formation of the Gothic as he sought to adapt it for political and personal reflections, in which the personal is always a reflection of the wider political moment. The Gothic identifies the points where personal and political resistance needs to take place. In one sense Dickens' version of the Gothic can historically be situated as working between the explorations of social repression which characterise the romantic era Gothic, and as anticipating the psychological reflections of the fin de siècle Gothic by authors such as Stevenson, Wilde, and Stoker. Within that historical arc, however, it is important to note that his is a Gothic which fulfils a particular purpose as he employs the Gothic to reflect on how the freedoms of the social reformist imagination need to be developed as a way of moving beyond corrupting institutions, historical legacies, and narrowly formed mentalities.

Bibliography

Adorno, Theodor W., 'On Dickens' *The Old Curiosity Shop*: A Lecture' in Rolf Tiedemann (ed.), *Notes to Literature*, Vol. 2 (New York: Columbia University Press, 1992), pp. 171–77.

Ballinger, Gill, 'Haunting the Law: Aspects of Gothic in Dickens's Fiction', *Gothic Studies*, 2008, Vol. 10, No. 2, 35–50.

Bowen, John, 'Charles Dickens and the Gothic' in Dale Townshend and Angela Wright (eds.), *The Cambridge History of the Gothic: Gothic in the Nineteenth Century* (Cambridge: Cambridge University Press, 2020), pp. 246–64.

Brooks, Peter, 'Repetition, and Return: *Great Expectations* and the Study of Plot', *New Literary History*, Spring 1980, Vol. 11, No. 3, 505–26.

Crofts, Matthew, 'Dickens's Gothic Double: *A Tale of Two Cities* and Watts Phillips's *The Dead Heart*', *Victoriographies*, 2018, Vol. 8, No. 3, 290–306.

Dardir, Ahmed Diaa, 'Fascination and Terror: Orientalism and the Return of the Repressed in *A Tale of Two Cities* and "A Christmas Tree"', *Dickens Quarterly*, September 2022, Vol. 39, No. 3, 338–58.

Dickens, Charles, *American Notes for General Circulation* (Harmondsworth: Penguin, 1985).

Dickens, Charles, *Great Expectations* (Harmondsworth: Penguin, 1982).

Dickens, Charles, *Bleak House* (Harmondsworth: Penguin, 1985).

Dickens, Charles, '*The Chimes*' in Michael Slater (ed.), *The Christmas Books*, Vol. 1 (Harmondsworth: Penguin, 1985), pp. 148–245.

Dickens, Charles, '*A Christmas Carol*' in Michael Slater (ed.), *The Christmas Books*, Vol. 1 (Harmondsworth: Penguin, 1985), pp. 45–134.

Dickens, Charles, '*The Haunted Man*' in Michael Slater (ed.), *The Christmas Books*, Vol. 2 (Harmondsworth: Penguin, 1985), pp. 244–353.

Dickens, Charles, *Oliver Twist* (Harmondsworth: Penguin, 1985).

Dickens, Charles, *Barnaby Rudge* (Harmondsworth: Penguin, 1986).

Dickens, Charles, *A Tale of Two Cities* (Harmondsworth: Penguin, 1989).

Dickens, Charles, '"Christmas Ghosts" from "A Christmas Tree"' in Paul Webb (Intro.), *The Signalman & Other Ghost Stories* (Stroud: Alan Sutton, 1990a), pp. 110–16.

Dickens, Charles, 'The Signalman' in Paul Webb (Intro.), *The Signalman & Other Ghost Stories* (Stroud: Alan Sutton, 1990b), pp. 1–13.

Dickens, Charles, 'The Black Veil' in Michael Slater (ed.), *Dickens' Journalism: Sketches by Boz and Other Early Papers 1833–39* (London: Dent, 1996a), pp. 359–68.

Dickens, Charles, 'Criminal Courts' in Michael Slater (ed.), *Dickens' Journalism: Sketches by Boz and Other Early Papers, 1833–39* (London: Dent, 1996b), pp. 194–98.

Dickens, Charles, 'A December Vision' in Michael Slater (ed.), *Dickens' Journalism: The Amusements of the People and Other Papers: Reports, Essays and Reviews 1834–1851* (London: Dent, 1996c), pp. 306–09.

Dickens, Charles, 'A Visit to Newgate' in Michael Slater (ed.), *Dickens' Journalism: Sketches by Boz and Other Early Papers 1833–39* (London: Dent, 1996d), pp. 199–210.

Dickens, Charles, 'Nurse's Stories' in Michael Slater and John Drew (eds.), *Dickens' Journalism: The Uncommercial Traveller and Other papers 1859–70* (London: Dent, 2000a), pp. 169–80.

Dickens, Charles, *The Old Curiosity Shop* (Harmondsworth: Penguin, 2000b).

Dickens, Charles, *Little Dorrit* (Harmondsworth: Penguin, 2003a).

Dickens, Charles, *The Pickwick Papers* (Harmondsworth: Penguin, 2003b).

Dickens, Charles and Wilkie Collins, *The Lazy Tour of Two Idle Apprentices* (New York: J.W. Lovell, 1884).

Federico, Annette R., 'Satis House', *Literary Imagination*, Vol. 21, No. 1, 63–76.

Freud, Sigmund, 'The Uncanny' in Albert Dickson (ed.), *Art and Literature: Jensen's 'Gradiva', Leonardo Da Vinci and Other Works* (Harmondsworth: Penguin, 1990), pp. 339–76.

Gillman, Susan K. and Robert L. Patten, 'Dickens: Doubles: Twins: Twains', *Nineteenth-Century Fiction*, March 1985, Vol. 39, No. 4, 441–56.

Glancy, Ruth, 'Christmas Books and Stories' in John Jordan, Robert L. Patten and Catherine Waters (eds.), *The Oxford Handbook of Charles Dickens* (Oxford: Oxford University Press, 2018), pp. 191–206.

Grass, Sean, *The Self in the Cell: Narrating the Victorian Prisoner* (London: Routledge, 2013).

Hollington, Michael, 'Boz's Gothic Gargoyles', *Dickens Quarterly*, 1999, Vol. 16, No. 3, 160–77.

Hutter, Albert D., 'Nation and Generation in *A Tale of Two Cities*' in Harold Bloom (ed.), *Modern Critical Interpretations: A Tale of Two Cities* (New York: Chelsea House, 1987), pp. 37–56.

Malone, Cynthia N., '"Flight" and "Pursuit": Fugitive Identity in *Bleak House*', *Dickens Studies Annual*, Spring 1990, Vol. 19, 107–24.

March, Eleanor, Dominique Moran, Matt Houlbrook, Yvonne Jewkes and Michaela Mahlberg, 'Defining the Carceral Characteristics of the "Dickensian Prison": A Corpus Stylistics Analysis of Dickens's Novels', *Victoriographies*, 2023, Vol. 13, No. 1, 15–41.

Marcus, Steven, 'Language into Structure: Pickwick Revisited', *Daedalus*, Winter 1972, Vol. 101, No. 1, 183–202.

Mighall, Robert, *A Geography of Victorian Gothic Fiction: Mapping History's Nightmares* (Oxford: Oxford University Press, 1999).

Mighall, Robert, 'Dickens and the Gothic' in David Paroissien (ed.), *Companion to Charles Dickens* (Hoboken: Wiley-Blackwell, 2009), pp. 81–96.

Milbank, Alison, *Daughters of the House: Modes of Gothic in Victorian Fic*tion (Basingstoke: Macmillan, 1992).

Simmons Jr., James R., '"Every Discernable Thing in It Was Covered with Dust and Mould": Radcliffe's Château-le-Blanc and Dickens's Satis House', *Dickensian*, Spring 1997, 11–12.

Slater, Michael, Editorial Comment on 'A December Vision' in Michael Slater (ed.), *Dickens' Journalism: The Amusements of The People and Other Papers: Reports, Essays and Reviews 1834–1851* (London: Dent, 1996), pp. 305–6.

Smajic, Srdjan, 'The Trouble with Ghost-Seeing: Vision, Ideology, and Genre in the Victorian Ghost Story', *English Literary History*, 2003, Vol. 70, No. 4, 1107–35.

Smith, Andrew, 'Colonial Ghosts: Mimicking Dickens in America' in Avril Horner and Sue Zlosnik (eds.), *Le Gothic* (Basingstoke: Palgrave, 2008), pp. 185–200.

Smith, Andrew, *The Ghost Story 1840–1920: A Cultural History* (Manchester: Manchester University Press, 2010).

Smith, Andrew, *Gothic Death 1740–1914: A Literary History* (Manchester: Manchester University Press, 2016).

Stahl D., John D., 'The Source and Significance of the Revenant in Dickens's "The Signal-Man"', *Dickens Studies Newsletter*, 11 (1980), 98–101.

Tambling, Jeremy, 'Prison-Bound: Dickens and Foucault', *Essays in Criticism*, 1986, Vol. xxxvi, No. 1, 11–31.

Trilling, Lionel, 'Little Dorrit', *The Kenyon Review*, Autumn 1953, Vol. 15, No. 4, 577–90.

Williams, Frederick S., *Our Iron Roads: Their History, Construction and Administration* (London: Frank Cass, 1968).

Cambridge Elements ≡

The Gothic

Dale Townshend
Manchester Metropolitan University
Dale Townshend is Professor of Gothic Literature in the Manchester Centre for Gothic Studies, Manchester Metropolitan University.

Angela Wright
University of Sheffield
Angela Wright is Professor of Romantic Literature in the School of English at the University of Sheffield and co-director of its Centre for the History of the Gothic.

Advisory Board

About the Series

Seeking to publish short, research-led yet accessible studies of the foundational 'elements' within Gothic Studies as well as showcasing new and emergent lines of scholarly enquiry, this innovative series brings to a range of specialist and non-specialist readers some of the most exciting developments in recent Gothic scholarship.

Cambridge Elements ☰

The Gothic

Elements in the Series

Printed in the United States
by Baker & Taylor Publisher Services